THE CHRIST OF HISTORY AND THE JESUS OF FAITH

THE CHRIST OF HISTORY AND THE JESUS OF FAITH

A Manifesto

DEREK TOVEY

Cover Image: My thanks to the Rev'd Sarah West <visiolectio.com> for the use of the block print image, "He is Risen".
The image depicts the encounter of Mary Magdalene with the Risen Jesus described in John 20:14-18, especially verse sixteen.

Copyright © 2024 by Derek Tovey

All rights reserved. No part of this book may be reproduced in any manner whatsoever without written permission except in the case of brief quotations embodied in critical articles and reviews.

First Printing, 2024

ISBN 978-0-473-70726-2

CONTENTS

Introduction: The Christ of History and the Jesus of Faith ~ A Manifesto   vii

One
The Resurrection of Jesus as an Item in Reconstructing the Historical Jesus   1

Two
The Search for the Historical Jesus: A Different Approach   8

Three
A Sketch of the Historical Jesus   29

Four
The Jesus of Faith and the Christ of History   55

Five
Conclusion: The Historical, Historic Christ as the Jesus of Faith   75

Appendix   83
Endnotes   95
Bibliography   119
About The Author   124

INTRODUCTION: THE CHRIST OF HISTORY AND THE JESUS OF FAITH ~ A MANIFESTO

Some years ago, I taught a course entitled "The Search for the Historical Jesus". The course's title occasioned some mirth amongst the support (office) staff of the theological institution in which I worked. "Is he still lost?", and other quips of like nature, were directed at me. The course designation derived from the English title of a famous book by Albert Schweitzer, *The Quest of the Historical Jesus*.[1] Contemporary terminology for this enterprise is, more sensibly, called "Historical Jesus Studies", or "Life-of-Jesus Research".

The "search" for Jesus, or the study of the historical Jesus, as it is has been carried on, and to a large extent still is currently, has thrown up a number of questions for me. Of course, the enterprise itself is beset by puzzles, and questions, that arise out of the nature of our source documents, and issues that they throw up, both individually and in comparison with one another. The task of history (or historiography) has its own set of questions and issues: and in the case of the historical Jesus, this is exacerbated, on the one hand, by the nature of the main source documents, and the paucity of other non-Christian sources, and, on the other hand, the increasing wealth of material (both primary and secondary) by way of possible background material for reconstructing the historical Jesus's environment.

But the questions I have are different: and perhaps in some respects, seemingly simplistic. They arise from a default perspective that has developed in, or rather was there from the outset of, historical Jesus research. That is the presumption that the historical Jesus is essentially other than the person who emerges from the pages of the New Testament (the gospels in particular). I expand on this in the chapters that follow, but in brief it is that the "historical Jesus" (the person who lived) and the "Christ of faith" (that is the Jesus that the early Christians proclaimed him to be) must be distinguished from one another. Somehow, the Christ of faith must be peeled away, as it were, so that the historian can recover the historical Jesus beneath the overlay of Christian faith.

One of the puzzles that this raises for me, particularly when faced with a reconstruction that peels away so much of supposed Christian overlay, is why the historical person that remains should be such a significant historical person? Why should the early Christians have pinned so much on him? Why did they, given his modest profile, attach so much significance to him? A further question is: if much of the material does not come from the historical Jesus, who were the geniuses that produced this material? Would it not be much more profitable to identify and study these persons (and as I shall argue below, I think we must think in terms of individuals rather than anonymous groups) rather than Jesus? But here I run the risk of running ahead of myself.

Why "a manifesto"? Anyone who is familiar with even a little of the research and writing on the historical Jesus, will know that it is a vast, and ever-expanding field of study. Many of the books written are not only very big, but are very erudite, and based on wide research and deep thinking. Many, if not most of them, are stimulating and enriching of an understanding of the "historical Jesus": they are very good, often well-expressed reconstructions. My own contribution here is very modest. And, though I do not wish to appear to dismiss this research and the reconstructions that abound, my offering may appear a little thin and perhaps even polemical. I do not intend it to be: but I do raise questions about some of the methods and approaches of some scholars (and some extremely substantial reconstructions of the historical Jesus). So what I have written is more in the nature of a "manifesto", in that it lays out arguments that are, perhaps, more asserted than argued. This is a kind of statement of thoughts, musings, and assumptions, or presuppositions about the data available, the nature of the gospels, the picture of Jesus that they present, than a deeply researched thesis. While I do engage with scholarship and a selection of scholars (much of the time in the footnotes), I am stating a position rather than arguing a case.

The first chapter was first delivered as a paper in a number of conference and seminar contexts. It has been very slightly revised. The remaining chapters have been written to try and bolster it with an examination of other issues (e.g. the nature of the source documents) and my own "sketch" of the historical Jesus as I would reconstruct him; as well as further reflections on the nature of history, and the role of the resurrection in a reconstruction of the historical Jesus.

All scholars who research the historical Jesus, barring a very few, agree that Jesus was a historical person. Where they disagree is over who that historical person was, what he was like, what he said and did. Above all, they disagree on how much we can trust the main sources we have for reconstructing a life of Jesus to give us a true picture of who he was. As these are sources that have come from early Christians who proclaimed Jesus as the Messiah, and indeed, more than that, as the Lord who is Son of God, and through his death brings us salvation, the suspicion arises that they have turned Jesus into someone he never was in his earthly life.

The sources themselves, as we have them, present their own puzzles. While I allude to some of these, you will have to look elsewhere for a full account of the many issues and problems that the New Testament documents raise: one of the major ones being, in relation to reconstructing the historical Jesus, what to make of the fact that three of them, the gospels of Matthew, Mark and Luke, appear to be related, or interrelated in some way, and John's Gospel is quite different.[2]

In 1958 a book written by Sir Edwyn Hoskyns and Noel Davey called *The Riddle of the New Testament*, appeared.[3] In it they wrote:

X – INTRODUCTION: THE CHRIST OF HISTORY AND THE JESUS OF FAITH ~ A MANIFESTO

> There is a riddle in the New Testament. And it is a riddle neither of literary criticism, nor of date and authorship, nor of the historicity of this or that episode. The riddle is a theological riddle, which is insoluble apart from the solution of an historical problem. What is the relation between Jesus of Nazareth and the primitive Christian church? That is the riddle. The New Testament documents, all of them, emerged from the primitive church. They reflected piety and encouraged faith. Was there, or was there not, a strict relationship between this rich piety and exuberant faith and the historical figure of Jesus of Nazareth? Did the life and death of Jesus control the life of the primitive church? or were his life and death submerged by a piety and faith wholly beyond his horizon?[4]

While my approach to this riddle is quite different from that of Hoskyns and Davey, it is that riddle that my manifesto addresses. My title, "The Christ of History and the Jesus of Faith", reverses the usual connections made between history and the Christ; theology, or faith, and the historical Jesus. What follows will, I hope, demonstrate why.

CHAPTER ONE

The Resurrection of Jesus as an Item in Reconstructing the Historical Jesus

The resurrection of Jesus needs to be the starting point for the study of the historical Jesus. This is not merely because there would be no "historical Jesus" without the witness of the first Christians. At the most, there may have been a notice of "a doer of wonderful works", or a wise man (as Josephus puts it), who was crucified; though I suspect that, without an ongoing movement attached to the person of Jesus, he would have sunk into obscurity.[5]

The reason the resurrection needs to be an item in reconstructing the historical Jesus is, first, because the resurrection as a catalyst for the early Christians' understanding of Jesus provides the best and most coherent explanation for why that understanding arose, given the time-frame within which it developed. Second, the early church's understanding of the historical Jesus is shaped by the resurrection, and its "event" character must be integrated into the understanding of the historical person Jesus, in order to accept the historical profile of Jesus promoted by the early church. This historical profile arises from a form of historical explanation, which I call "theologised history".

Of course, to claim that the resurrection needs to be considered as an item in reconstructing the historical Jesus is a claim that goes against much historical Jesus scholarship. The resurrection is often bracketed out of consideration as something that lies beyond historical inquiry. The comment by Joachim Gnilka may be taken as representative: "The story of the resurrection of the crucified one from the dead is no longer part of the earthly history of Jesus of Nazareth."[6] Furthermore, "the Jesus of history" has been split off from "the Christ of faith" with what I would consider to be some perverse outcomes for the practice of New Testament historiography.[7] I explore an aspect of this in an appendix.

There are two warrants for considering the resurrection an item in reconstructing the historical Jesus. The first is that the original disciples based their claims for identifying this historical person Jesus, as the Christ (the Messiah) and as they went on to claim "the Son of God", on the fact that, though he had been crucified and buried, God raised him up. They knew this because Jesus had appeared to them, in some form that convinced them that he was alive; that he had been resurrected from the dead. One of the earliest testimonies to this is, of course, Paul's statement – seemingly referring to a tradition he has received – in 1 Corinthians 15:3–8 "that [Jesus, the Christ] was raised on the third day in accordance with the scriptures, and that he appeared to Cephas, then to the twelve. Then he appeared to more than five hundred brothers and sisters at one time, most of whom are still alive, though some have died. Then he appeared to James, then to all the apostles. Last of all, as to one untimely born, he appeared also to me".[8] Without taking time to debate how we might exegete all of this, I simply observe that Paul appears to set these appearances down as a series of "facts". They are, to use the speech-act language of Mary Louise Pratt, the "appropriateness conditions" whereby the truth of the assertion that God raised Jesus from the dead, is secured.[9] Some might be correlated with the traditions later recorded in the gospels of appearances to the disciples. These, and other texts, are part of a textual testimony across the New Testament writings to the resurrection of Jesus (often attributed to the action of God).[10]

Hermann Samuel Reimarus (1694–1768), credited with beginning the process of modern Jesus research, maintained that the disciples stole Jesus's body from the tomb, and then, after fifty days (when the body could no longer be identified), proclaimed his resurrection and imminent return. In his view, Jesus saw himself as a political messiah and the kingdom of God he proclaimed was a political kingdom to be established here on earth. When Jesus sent his disciples out on a mission to the towns and villages of Judea and Galilee (see Mark 6:7–13), he provided no teaching on the nature of the kingdom of God. Therefore, he must have expected the disciples to promote the commonly expected understanding of the Messiah, namely one who would drive out the Roman overlords. Jesus and his disciples accordingly expected, when they reached Jerusalem, that the people would rise up and help them establish the kingdom. This did not happen and Jesus was instead crucified and his disciples were dispersed in fear and despondency.

What happened next was that the disciples decided that rather than go back to their former way of life, they would "resurrect" Jesus as "a spiritual saviour of the human race". Reimarus attributes a mercenary motive to the disciples for this move: they would live off the proceeds that came from the adherents they attracted to this concocted faith.[11] His deception theory has mostly been rejected, but his method of separating out what Jesus preached and thought from what the disciples, and the early church, taught and thought about Jesus post-resurrection, has been widely followed; and one might even say is standard practice amongst researchers into the historical Jesus.

There is a sense in which, if we are to discount the remembered history of Jesus put out by the early Christians, Reimarus's thesis was at least honest, as it put the creation of much, if not most, of the Jesus material onto the early church. Nevertheless, in my opinion, Reimarus overplayed his hand. The time-frame required for the development of such an elaborate, yet essentially coherent story as the church's story of Jesus is far more than allowed for in a fifty day period. Especially when the accounts all suggest that the disciples were completely blind-sided by the death of Jesus.[12] Of course, the story of Jesus developed over decades, but at the heart of it lies a question: what was it about Jesus that made the early church settle upon him as the centre of this story? One of the puzzles, it seems to me, that lies at the heart of many of the reconstructions of Jesus, and particularly those that strip away much of what is reported that Jesus said and did as creations of the early church, is "Why Jesus"? How is it possible for the geniuses that created the traditions about Jesus to remain so much in the background, so anonymous, so self-effacing, in favour of promoting a man who was relatively obscure, who did not say very much, nor do very much, but somehow gets proclaimed as "Messiah and Lord"?

Let's recall that Paul, one of the earliest witnesses to belief in the resurrection, and the one who passed on the tradition of resurrection appearances, was a self-confessed opponent of the Jesus movement. What possessed him to buy into a story manufactured by a bunch of people whom he opposed? John Dominic Crossan rejects the parable of the Good Samaritan as having been told by Jesus on the basis of its singular attestation, and John P. Meier, an otherwise careful scholar who accepts much of the Jesus material as coming from him, does likewise.[13] The question is, if Jesus did not tell that marvellous story, who did? I cannot believe that it is the creation of an anonymous group. For me, the question presses in: if Jesus did not create this and other parables, isn't it more worthwhile to search for the one who did?[14] It seems to me far too easy for traditions to be sloughed off onto the early church (without asking questions about who these people were), and leaving behind a Jesus who is denuded of meaningful significance.

Markus Bockmuehl in a chapter on the resurrection, writes this:

> [E]ven the more mainstream participants in the late twentieth-century 'historical Jesus' bonanza have tended to avoid the subject of the resurrection – usually on the pretext that this is solely a matter of 'faith' or of 'theology', about which no self-respecting historian could possibly have anything to say. Precisely that scholarly silence, however, renders a good many recent 'historical Jesus' studies methodologically hamstrung, and unable to deliver what they promise. Quite what transpired on that third day after the crucifixion is of course a complex question...Nevertheless, it is a matter of historical record that *something* happened – and that this changed the course of world history like no other event before or since.[15]

Granted that the resurrection, on the New Testament evidence, can be understood in at least a couple of ways (that is, as a bodily resurrection, or as a movement of Jesus directly to the right hand of God),[16] it is that *something* that was the catalyst for the early church's understanding of Jesus. I think it was an objective event, or perhaps more properly a series of events:[17] even though the exact nature of it/them cannot be precisely captured. Hence, I would argue that it is the event(s) of the resurrection that provided the stimulus for identifying this historical figure, Jesus, as the Christ, and "Son of God". Much of this understanding was retrojected onto the historical Jesus, because this event put the historical Jesus into a new light.

The question of course arises: was this understanding of the historical Jesus a legitimate understanding of his life, his character and being? Are we placing a theological, or Christological dress upon an historical person which does not belong? Many would say, "Yes".

Here I need to change tack and make a pitch for a different philosophy of history. At heart is the matter of the interpretive function of history. In other words, beyond the descriptive function of history: "this is what happened" if you will, there is the interpretive function: "this is what this event signifies". Since the Enlightenment, interpretations that derive from supernatural causation have been ruled out of court. This means that the New Testament witness immediately falls foul of the "canons of modern historiography". The claim, this is what happened: Jesus appeared to Peter, to James, to five hundred people (with Paul chiming in, "and he even appeared to me, the former persecutor of the church"), and this is how we interpret it (or to put it differently: this is the significance we place upon it): God raised Jesus up, God has declared Jesus both Lord and Messiah, this is all ruled out of court as an acceptable historical explanation.

Why is this explanation of the significance of this historical figure, Jesus, put forward? What is the reason for placing this kind of an interpretation upon Jesus? It is the result of the resurrection, and the impact of this experience (an experience of an event, in the true historical sense) upon the disciples' understanding of who Jesus was, and is, and of the meaning of his life and death. Larry Hurtado, in his book *How on Earth Did Jesus Become a God?* makes a strong case for the early development, within an understanding of Jewish monotheism, of the view that Jesus was divine, alongside of God.[18] This rules out, in my view, many of the evolutionary theories that are put forward that see the early Christian belief as deriving from either Jewish ideas of resurrection, or Graeco-Roman ideas about humans who become gods, and so forth.[19] How this explanatory interpretation of the historical person relates to that person's history must be the subject of further work.

Nevertheless, although we may wish to describe this as a theologically-motivated historical explanation, it remains an historical explanation nonetheless. The test is whether or not it makes good sense of the data. Does it provide, if not the only, at least a plausible reconstruction of the historical Jesus, especially taking into account the kind of effect he had on his followers and the ongoing movement?[20] Does it best explain the abiding significance of this historical person? Does it explain how he has been remembered? Does it account for why an obscure first-century Galilean Jew, who may or may not have been a wonderful storyteller, who may or may not have performed exorcisms (most think he probably did) or other miraculous deeds, has become a towering figure of historic proportions? There is not a single answer to those questions; and perhaps there never will be. But whatever answer is given, the resurrection must be woven into the story: and I would maintain it must be taken account of in terms of the historical reconstruction of Jesus's life and death.

CHAPTER TWO

The Search for the Historical Jesus: A Different Approach

The four canonical gospels are our best, fullest and most useful sources for reconstructing the historical Jesus. This is a widely held consensus amongst scholars, and certainly they are the most used in scholarship.[21] Generally, the three Synoptic Gospels (Matthew, Mark, and Luke) are considered the most useful, and are the canonical gospels most widely used. The Gospel of John is considered less reliable, mostly because its presentation of Jesus is so different from the other three. It is often set aside completely by scholars seeking to reconstruct the historical Jesus, but I think this is a mistake.[22] In more recent times, John's Gospel has been rehabilitated as an historical source.

One of the perverse outcomes, in my opinion, of the split between the "Jesus of history" and the "Christ of faith", generated by the suspicion of the gospel writings as confessional, and "biased" presentations of Jesus, is the attempt to get behind the gospel material to recover the "authentic" Jesus, and the data that may be taken as most "primitive" and, therefore, most reliable as a source for what Jesus actually said and did. This has led, since the Second World War, to the development of "criteria of authenticity" in an attempt to single out what may be securely accepted as reliable historical ("authentic") material from material that arises out of the interests of the early church.[23]

Now it is entirely the case that the material in the gospels themselves present historians with puzzles and with the need to sort out from the material which data provide information from which a reliable (in the sense of approximating to what may have been the case) reconstruction may be made. To begin with, the relationship among the three Synoptic Gospels, and to a lesser extent the Gospel of John, raise questions of the dependence of one upon the other (or the independence of their material, to put it the other way). Furthermore, when it comes to the question of sources behind the gospels, the presence of the "double tradition", that is material common to Matthew and Luke but not found in Mark, commonly designated as "Q", suggests that they are drawing on prior source material which may come from oral tradition, or a mix of oral and written sources.[24]

Nonetheless, it is my contention that in the task of historical reconstruction we must take the gospels as they are. *They* are the sources to which we have access today, and we must determine a way to use them as historical sources as they stand. We cannot look for sources behind them, or attempt to discern within them the oral traditions that preceded their production. This is not to deny that there was a process of oral transmission of Jesus tradition. In my opinion, one of the best accounts of the nature of this oral tradition has been given by James D.G. Dunn.[25] The existence of the double tradition within Matthew and Luke, commonly referred to as "Q", is further evidence that a hypothesis of an orally transmitted body of Jesus tradition is valid and a possible explanation for some of the material found in the Synoptic Gospels. It might also be said that material in John's Gospel (think, for instance, of the feeding of the five thousand in John 6, or the healing of the royal official's son in John 4), points to the likelihood that this Gospel is in touch with a (pre-Synoptic) oral tradition.

However, in the end, *what we have now as sources* are these traditions as they have been gathered into the written form of the gospels. Furthermore, the search for oral traditions remains a largely hypothetical and speculative exercise. Even Dunn frequently refers to the fact that getting to the oral tradition is a reconstructive (my word) exercise.[26] Moreover, wherever the evangelists obtained their material from, they themselves have played a big part in determining the manner that the tradition has been shaped and handed down to us.[27]

If the advent of Redaction Criticism (the examination of how the evangelists edited and brought together their material) has alerted us to the fact that the evangelists were "authors" in their own right with their own particular theological interests and tendencies shaping the material, Narrative Criticism has extended this into an understanding of the dynamics and strategies by which they have presented their stories of Jesus as (more or less) carefully constructed, plotted, and integrated narratives. I have attempted to show how this is the case as regards to the gospels of John and Mark.[28] This may be seen, in the case of Mark for instance, in the way the evangelist has plotted his story through the use of narrative "inclusios" (Mark 8:22–26; 10:46–52), and repetitions (two feeding miracles in 6:30–44; 8:1–10; three attempts to teach the disciples about the character of his messiahship in 8:31–38; 9:30–37; 10:32–45).[29] One might note how the inclusios (involving in each case the healing of a blind man) bracket the three attempts to teach the disciples about Jesus's messiahship, raising a question over the progress, or lack of it, in the disciples' understanding of this.

The gospel writers played a major role in creating the image of Jesus that we have today. The character of the literature they produced is such that, in my view, we should regard the gospels as the work of creative individuals rather than the work of a community. Keith Bosley, in an Introduction to *The Kalevala*, on the origins of this Finnish national epic writes, "A village might claim a 'singing family': though the Western world may still dream of noble savages composing in committee, oral epic was the preserve of a talented few."[30] Even the Yugoslavian singers, whose epic poems were captured by Parry and Lord, were individuals who "created" the songs.

In his book, *The Singer of Tales*, Albert Lord has this to say about the production of the songs: "…every performance is a separate song; for every performance is unique, and every performance bears the signature of its poet singer."[31] Later he states that "the moment of composition is the performance", and goes on shortly after to state, "The oral poet is composer. Our singer of tales is a composer of tales. Singer, performer, composer, and poet are one under different aspects *but at the same time*. Singing, performing, composing are facets of the same act."[32] Furthermore, he later states that the singer is the author, and a single author at that: "...the author of an oral epic, that is, the text of a performance, is the performer, the singer before us. The author of any of our texts, unless an editor has tampered with it, is the man who dictated, sang, chanted, or otherwise gave expression to it. A performance is unique; it is a creation, not a reproduction, and it can therefore have only one author."[33]

While the gospel writers had a major part to play in bringing together the material we may refer to as "Jesus tradition", they did not themselves create this out of their imagination. They did use sources, many of them oral (though examination of the Synoptic Gospels suggests that Matthew and Luke also used Mark). However, rather than drawing upon a long tradition of anonymously created small units of tradition (as proposed by the form critics), I think that the evangelists received their material far more directly from the apostles and eyewitnesses to Jesus's life and ministry. And they themselves were the "single author" responsible for the final work that we now have.

We need to take far more seriously the testimony and traditional ascriptions of the early generation of Christians regarding the genesis of the gospels. An early and important witness to this genesis is in the writings of Papias. Though he receives the information at second hand, it is worth quoting what he says here as relayed by Eusebius, who writes: "For our present purpose we must add to his statements already quoted above a tradition concerning Mark, who wrote the Gospel, that has been set forth in these words":

> And the elder used to say this: "Mark, having become Peter's interpreter, wrote down accurately everything he remembered, though not in order, of the things either said or done by Christ. For he neither heard the Lord nor followed him, but afterward, as I said, followed Peter, who adapted his teachings as needed but had no intention of giving an ordered account of the Lord's sayings. Consequently Mark did nothing wrong in writing down some things as he remembered them, for he made it his one concern not to omit anything that he heard or to make any false statement in them."
>
> Such, then, is the account given by Papias with respect to Mark. But with respect to Matthew the following is said: "So Matthew composed the oracles in the Hebrew language and each person interpreted them as best he could."[34]

Thus the testimony of Papias, for instance, that Mark was the "interpreter" of Peter, may mean that Mark's main source for much of the tradition was Peter, and what we have are Peter's reminiscences or remembrance of Jesus.[35]

Luke's Gospel begins with the statement that he has written his account in the wake of many other attempts to write "an orderly account" (NRSV) recording events "as they were handed down to us by those who from the beginning were eyewitnesses and servants of the word" (see Luke 1:1–4). In the Acts of the Apostles, Luke gives us an account in which seven deacons are appointed to ensure that the Hellenistic Jewish widows did not continue to get overlooked in the care that the early church extended to widows (see Acts 6:1–7). "The Twelve" give as a reason why these men should be appointed that fact that they themselves should not "neglect the word of God" (v. 2). I think that this means, in part at least, that the Twelve saw their main role as preserving and passing on the teaching of Jesus, and no doubt reflecting upon and framing their proclamation of who Jesus was and is in the light of their scriptures.[36] As an aside, and admittedly as pure speculation, I sometimes wonder how much the "many priests" who "became obedient to the faith" (Acts 6:7) contributed to the process of scriptural reflection upon the significance of Jesus. Papias's further comment about Matthew compiling "the oracles in the Hebrew language; but everyone interpreted them as he was able", may well be a hint that behind the gospels of Matthew and Luke, at least, lie a document (perhaps a form of Q?) that contained sayings of Jesus in Aramaic.[37]

Papias also commented about preferring the "living voice" over written documents. This may be understood as testimony to the fact that individuals were the bearers of the tradition (a point that Dunn himself makes), and that transition from oral testimony from particular individuals to the written account may be closer than often thought.[38] In this regard, we may need to revisit the late dating of the Gospels (that is mostly post-70 CE, and thirty to forty years after Jesus's death), as has traditionally been maintained.[39] As an aside, we should note that Papias's preference for "the living voice" over "books" (or written accounts) is made in the context of the fact that written accounts were also widely desired by the early Christian communities, otherwise it is unlikely that the gospels would have been copied and circulated. In other words, written gospels were produced and copied because they were valued as bearers of Jesus tradition alongside of, and as well as, orally transmitted Jesus tradition. Papias's preference may be a testimony to the importance of the bearers of the tradition which formed the gospels, rather than a denial of the importance attributed to written accounts. We should not overlook the irony that Papias himself expresses his preference for oral tradition in the context of a written work.

The gospels, then, remain for us the primary source of data for the historical Jesus.[40] However, none of this should be taken as meaning that they are themselves historical accounts. They are certainly not purely historical accounts, as they have been shaped and developed according to the design and interests of the evangelists. They provide the data for historical accounts. The history of the historical Jesus is something produced by the historian alongside of, and out of, the gospels. What is needed is a method of using the gospel data for the purposes of historical reconstruction. What is also needed is a philosophy of history that can accommodate material that falls outside of the (normally accepted) canons of secular historiography. To that question I now turn.

The Nature of History, Historiography and the Historical Jesus.

In the English language, the word "history" is used in two senses. First, it denotes events that happened in the past. Second, it denotes accounts of events that have happened in the past. In this book, I am using "history" in the second sense. That is, when I refer to history, I mean historiography: "history" in the sense of events that happened in the past has gone, we can only reconstruct the events from what comes to us either in oral testimony, or written documents. That is, "history" is basically the discourse produced by the historian in reconstructing the past using testimony, or written documents. Historians, of course, also use artefacts from the past: coins, statues, material obtained from archaeological digs, or uncovered by such work, such as, for example, the remains of a building or some structure.

History, or historiography, as a reconstructive exercise is also an exercise in interpretation. Every event or historical "fact" is also an interpreted event or "fact". This is the case even with eyewitness testimony: what we have is the event as the witness saw it, and as he or she describes it, together with whatever interpretation they put upon it (not to mention factors such as whether their memory serves them well, how much they have "understood" the event, and so forth). Artefacts, of course, are mute, and must be interpreted by the archaeologist or the historian as they analyse the artefact, and draw conclusions from their analysis. Occasionally, one reads a New Testament scholar who will say something along the lines of "such and such an account is not the same as if we had a video recording of the event". Such comments, I suggest, tend to forget the fact that even a video recording needs to be interpreted by the viewer (leaving aside that we would only have a record of what the video camera captured, not of what happened out of shot, as it were). A fully rounded understanding of an event would probably require it to be captured by dozens, if not hundreds of cameras. Although we may be able to determine the intentions of an author in a more-or-less faithful manner, even dealing with written records is an interpretive exercise.

This is to say that "history" is not only an exercise in reconstruction, it is also an exercise in interpretation. It also calls for what R. G. Collingwood has called "historical imagination".[41] So producing an historical account, a reconstruction of an historical event, is a self-involving exercise. The historian invests her, or himself, in the reconstruction, along with her or his biases, worldview, philosophical outlook, and personality. We are long past the positivistic view of historiography, whereby the historian took up some supposedly objective, neutral standpoint. This is not to say that history is only something that arises out of an historian's perspective, and that the "facts of history" (as E. H. Carr calls them) are entirely the creation of a given historical account or interpretation.[42]

When it comes to the "search for the historical Jesus", John Dominic Crossan complains that *"Historical Jesus research* is becoming something of a scholarly bad joke."[43] He says this because of the many different images or reconstructions of Jesus that have been appearing in recent years. This, however, is to be expected: and, in my opinion, no apologies or sense of discomfort need arise. Different historians will arrive at different interpretations of the data; they will use different methods to assess the reliability of the data; they may choose to select different "facts of history", and even deny certain "facts" as genuinely having happened (this is especially the case when dealing with data relating to Jesus).

So how do we determine how to do the reconstruction? How do we determine what are the "facts" – what criteria shall we use for determining historicity? There are particular difficulties in working with the gospels. There is, for a start, the question of the relationship among them. There is the question of their nature, which is as documents written to persuade the reader towards a certain understanding of Jesus (what is often called in scholarship, their "theological tendencies"). They present a certain understanding of Jesus that moves them from the realm of history, into a theological perspective on Jesus and his significance. The theological perspective of the gospels I shall return to below.

Given that the gospels provide the raw materials for constructing a history of Jesus, our approach should be to construct this history out of, and above the gospels. It is not to dig behind, or to attempt to uncover from within the "historical" figure beneath the theological overlay, as it were. We should aim to construct what W. B. Gallie might call a "followable story".[44] That is, out of the data before the historian, he or she constructs a narrative that draws together the contingent events into a "teleologically guided" and coherent account. Gallie states:

> [H]istory, like all stories and all imaginative literature, is as much a journey as an arrival, as much an approach as a result. Again, every genuine work of history is read in this way because its subject matter is felt to be worth following–through contingencies, accidents, setbacks, and all the multifarious details of its development.[45]

In an historical narrative, of course, this account must be based on evidence, and be plausible: thus is must be a narrative that is congruent with the beliefs, customs, mores and social conditions of the age in which it is set, but it must be coherent in that it draws together the evidence in a way that makes sense of the before and after of an event.

Hence, a "followable story" of the life and ministry of Jesus must place him plausibly and coherently into early first-century Palestine, and Second-Temple Jewish life and thought, as well as explain why the movement continued beyond his crucifixion, and developed the way it did. Much historical Jesus research concentrates upon the first part of this enterprise: that is placing Jesus plausibly into his context, but fails to explain, or struggles to account for the ongoing effects of his life and ministry. This area of enquiry is what Jonathan Bernier identifies as a "Fourth Quest": that is, it focuses "upon dispensing with the myth of a rupture between Jesus and Christianity".[46]

Bernier's own method (apart from his philosophy of history, which he describes as critical realism) is to make inferences from the data in the gospels, and from these inferences to draw conclusions that may be deemed plausible explanations of the data. For instance, from references to disciples of Jesus in what he calls the "Bethany/Bethphage complex" (that is passages in the gospels that refer to people in the region of Bethany/Bethphage) he infers that Jesus had followers ("recruited followers", even) in this region, for example, Mary, Martha and Lazarus (see Luke 10: 38–41; John 11:1), and an unknown owner of a donkey (Mark 11:1–7//Matt 21:1–7//Luke 19:29–35).[47] As Bethany/Bethphage did not feature as a known centre for Christians in the early church, it is unlikely that these traditions were post-Easter inventions of the early Christians.

He bolsters these inferences and plausible conclusions with reference to what he calls "the Missional Complex" (see Matt 10:5–15; Mark 6:6–13; Luke 9:1–6; cf. Luke 10:1–12), that is, the sending out on mission of the twelve, and the seventy, or seventy-two.[48] The inference being that this mission may well have included contact with those who became followers of Jesus in the region of Bethany/Bethphage during the ministry of Jesus. Furthermore, noting that John's Gospel records Jesus making several trips to Jerusalem (discussed by Bernier under the heading of a "Festival Complex"), it may well have been on one of these trips that the recruitment of followers in Bethany/Bethphage took place.[49]

This method of drawing inferences from the data leading to plausible conclusions, or a plausible reconstruction from the data, seems to me to be an entirely reasonable way of proceeding. It leads to an historical reconstruction that is thorough and plausible, and every bit as reliable as, if not more reliable than, a reconstruction based upon criteria of authenticity. Bernier's approach, it seems to me, fits with the "two salient features" of Gallie's historical understanding, namely,

> first that our basic attitude is that of following the historian's narrative–in the same broad sense in which we follow a game or story–across all manner of real-life contingencies and surprises to its broadly fore-known conclusion; and secondly that we are quite prepared to have any incident on the road to that conclusion explained to us, or justified, not simply by the production of appropriate evidence, but by all manner of general considerations and arguments.[50]

It seems to me that this is essentially the type of procedure followed by, for example, E.P. Sanders in his *The Historical Figure of Jesus*.[51] By and large, Sanders seeks to place Jesus into his first-century Jewish context. He does this by presenting the actions of Jesus (e.g. his miracles) and teaching against the backdrop of Jewish analogies and examples by way of comparison. The result is a reasonably broad-brush portrait building upon a set of "almost indisputable facts" that form the framework for developing a more rounded picture of Jesus.[52] While Sanders accepts the validity of the "criteria of authenticity", with some reservations, it seems to me that he very rarely resorts to determining the historicity of an item with reference to these. This is in marked contrast to John P. Meier's approach in his magisterial five volumes on the historical Jesus, *A Marginal Jew: Rethinking the Historical Jesus*.[53] Meier subjects every pericope (passage) and item he uses to reconstruct the historical Jesus to a meticulous and exhaustive examination using the criteria of authenticity. For a critique of the criteria of authenticity, see my appendix (pp. 84-88).

I mention Bernier and Sanders as examples of scholars whose approach tends towards presenting a "followable story", by presenting an overall picture of Jesus that seeks to provide an attempt to bring together an explanation of Jesus that sets him within his Jewish context, while also attempting to provide a link with the movement that remained after his death.[54] While Bernier's approach is more the outline of a method than a full-blown account of the historical Jesus, one expects that his historical Jesus would be more closely aligned with the movement that followed than Sanders's approach suggests. Sanders is more sceptical of the material in the gospels than I expect Bernier is.

My own reading of a wide range of scholars who have written on the historical Jesus persuades me that it is possible to construct a synthesis of the historical Jesus which would draw together a wide-range of perspectives and approaches into a picture that is coherent and reasonably widely established. I shall attempt that synthesis in the next chapter.

History and historical significance: not only what happened, but what it means.

History is not simply a matter of detailing the event by laying out what actions, decisions, pronouncements by the actors (or characters) contributed to the event and its development and outcome. It is also a matter of providing an account of the significance of the event.[55] It is one thing to say that a man was crucified, and provide an account of how this event came about. It is another thing to say why he was crucified. It is one thing to say that after the death of this man, his followers, though initially cast into confusion and despair, regrouped and formed a movement based on the claim that God had raised the crucified man from death. It is another thing to account for why this should have come about. What then, in the light of the man's death by crucifixion and the subsequent claim of his resurrection is the significance of this? What is the *historical significance* of this event: now to be understood as a crucifixion–(claimed) resurrection complex.

In other words, the event calls for interpretation. The interpretation is based not merely upon the production of evidence, but, as Gallie says, "all manner of general considerations and arguments". In the case of the historical Jesus, the question is what significance, and what interpretation should be placed upon his life and death? What is the historical significance of his ministry, and the crucifixion that brought that ministry to an end? The first Christians placed an interpretation upon the life and death of Jesus that appears to place their claims for the historical significance of Jesus largely outside of the realms of historical inquiry: it is a significance that can only be grasped by faith. They base these claims upon the proclamation that God raised Jesus from the dead. The resurrection is a surprising eventuality for the history of a human life: and, as far as historical inquiry is concerned, takes the narrative into "unfollowable" territory.

But should it? These are claims that are made for an historical person, by people who knew him as an historical person, and whose claims for his historical significance are, as far as can be ascertained, made in good faith. They do not aim to deceive (as Reimarus thought), nor, they claim, are they following "cleverly devised myths" (2 Peter 1:16, NRSV).[56] Nevertheless, their claims for Jesus as an historical person must be, and are, put to the test by historians. The difficulty that historians have had, since the time of Reimarus, and in the light of the rise of modern historiographical methods and standards, is in finding a *modus operandum* that can deal with an event that involves the transcendent, or that cannot be contained within the canons of secular history. But when the impact of that historical life, and the traces left in the movement that arose from it, seem to be most plausibly explained by taking seriously the claims of the early Christians for the historical significance of the historical Jesus, what then? It is my contention that historiographical discourse must find a way to treat this seriously: and to construct a plausible account of that life and what flowed from it. In what follows, I attempt to address this question.

Theological meaning and historical significance.

We have seen that history is a matter of event and interpretation of the event. In fact, under my understanding of history as basically historical discourse, that is writing or speaking about events of the past, history is a matter of reconstructing an event (from the data available from the past) and also providing an interpretation of that event, and in particular, drawing out the meaning or the historical significance of that event.

When it comes to the historical Jesus, the historical significance of Jesus, as far as the gospel and other early Christian data is concerned, is couched in theological language, and brings out an historical significance that is theologically motivated and informed. We might also say it is confessionally generated. James D. G. Dunn picks up Martin Kähler's distinction between *historische* ("historical") and *"geschichtliche"* ("historic"). He writes:

> *Historie* he [Kähler] understands as merely historical, the bare data, independent of any significance that might be placed upon them. *Geschichte*, on the other hand, denotes history in its significance, historical events and persons that attract attention by reason of the influence they have exercised. The point is that the Gospels present the *geschictliche Christus*, Jesus seen in his significance.[57]

Dunn's further point (made earlier in the chapter from which this above quotation is taken) is vitally important. He states that the only Jesus we have access to, as far as using the Gospels (and New Testament material generally) for our historical reconstructions is concerned, is the Jesus *as remembered by the disciples, and those who knew Jesus*. He follows what I have quoted above by writing this:

> ...there is no historical Jesus to be found in the Gospels, only the historic figure evident to us through the influence he exercised on his disciples, through the impact he made on them in calling them into discipleship.[58]

This was, indeed, noted as long ago as 1962 when N. A. Dahl succinctly wrote: "We do not escape the fact that we know Jesus only as the disciples remembered him."[59]

This is both the reality and the problem. What we have is remembered significance, and data that comes from the testimony of committed persons, committed to a particular understanding of the historic significance of Jesus. This is why for two hundred years or more, much of the material we have for historical reconstruction has been sloughed off onto the early church as their creation, out of their needs and interests.

But the question is: in terms of historical (or, historic) significance, do their claims capture well the significance that should attach to the historical person, Jesus? Are their claims a true historical reflection of who this person actually was? Or are we finding a created "Christ" out of an historical personage who was quite different, and cannot have the historic significance that the early Christians attached to him?

It is obvious, from even a cursory glance at the literature that different researchers and historians will come to different conclusions on this. These conclusions will be driven by many considerations that include what data the historian will determine can be plausibly attributed to Jesus, and the particular perspective, and it has to be said "faith commitment" (and this includes a "no faith" commitment) that the historian brings to his or her reconstruction. So there will be different determinations of the historic significance of Jesus.

My argument here is, not that there should not be different determinations, but that a particular determination (one that arises from theological commitments) should not be ruled out of order *tout court* simply on those grounds. To put it another way, there is a form of history that may be called "theological history" which must be permitted to stand on equal ground along with other forms of history.[60]

The question then becomes: which form of history, and precisely which form of theological history, makes good and plausible sense of the data on the historical Jesus (and thus provides a good and plausible reconstruction) *and provides a plausible and adequate account of the historic significance of Jesus*? This must not only include placing Jesus plausibly in his historical context, but also plausibly explaining the historic significance of Jesus as the early church came to see it. This is, I think, at the heart of the call for the "Fourth Quest" that Jonathan Bernier puts forward.

This is why I maintain that the resurrection (the accounts and belief in the resurrection) must be made part of the reconstruction of the historical Jesus. Are the claims made by the early Christians for the historic significance of the historical Jesus valid? I believe they are, and I shall expand on this below. N.T. Wright in his big book *The Resurrection of the Son of God*, claims that Gospel accounts of the resurrection, and thus the early Christian claim for the historic significance of Jesus (by a process of inference to the best explanation) is the best explanation of the data.[61] Dale Allison objects to his position, and states that "best explanation" is too certain and, one might say, "dogmatic" (my term) a claim.[62] He has a point: but let us say that such an explanation must be allowed to stand as an historical explanation alongside others as a good and plausible explanation. Each historian, each reader will decide whether or not it is the best (that is, *most* plausible) explanation.

Explaining Belief in the Resurrection.

There are two main ways, I suggest, by which an explanation for the early Christians' belief in the resurrection is provided. One is that it is part of a process whereby the Christians developed these beliefs under the influence of, or out of reflection upon and adaptation of Jewish and Greco-Roman beliefs in the afterlife and the concept of resurrection.

Whatever the catalyst for the rise of these beliefs (whether a series of hallucinations, or something else), this explanation is largely an exercise in the history of ideas.[63]

The difficulty this type of explanation faces is the sheer rapidity by which the early Christians' belief in, and proclamation of, the resurrection of Jesus occurred. Generally, the impression given by this type of explanation is that belief in Jesus's resurrection grew and developed over a period of decades. This cannot be sustained. It has been shown that devotion to Jesus as Christ and Lord was a very early phenomenon. As Larry Hurtado has written:

> Perhaps within only a few days or weeks of his crucifixion, Jesus' followers were circulating the astonishing claim that God had raised him from death and had installed him in heavenly glory as Messiah and the appointed vehicle of redemption. Moreover, and still more astonishing, these claims were accompanied by an emerging pattern of devotional practices in which Jesus figured with an unprecedented centrality.[64]

Hurtado argues that a variety of worship activities written about, and alluded to, in the New Testament writings, show that the early Christians worshiped Jesus, alongside God (the Father), and gave him a divine status, equal to God, and not accorded to any other beings, either spiritual or human. Hurtado gives the designation "binitarian" to the shape of this worship, meaning that the early Christians accorded this status to Jesus and this worship while remaining within the parameters of Jewish monotheism. This is a "mutation" within ancient Jewish monotheism. He writes:

> ...Jesus is incorporated into an exclusivist pattern of devotion in which there is room for only *one God and one Lord* (e.g. 1 Cor. 8:5–6). So, what we have is a binitarian, exclusivist monotheism, able to accommodate Jesus, but disdainful of any other god or lord as rightful recipient of devotion.[65]

The reason for this rapid and strongly attested elevation of a crucified human to this position of exaltation and as the recipient of the early Christians' devotion and worship, Hurtado attributes to revelatory experiences that made a profound impression on these Christians. These revelatory experiences centre on the resurrection appearances.[66]

The problem with Hurtado's argument here, in my opinion, is that it tends to suggest, or give the impression at least, that these revelatory experiences were purely subjective experiences that prompted the early Christians to adopt a new set of convictions about Jesus. It is true that the resurrection appearances were subjective in the sense that these were experiences of the risen Jesus that came to selected individuals, or groups (on one occasion five hundred at one time), and to which they bore witness. When Paul lists the resurrection appearances in 1 Corinthians 15: 5–8, he includes himself as one to whom the risen Christ appeared. We assume that in this case, Paul's experience was of a visionary nature.[67] Does this mean the others saw the risen Christ in a similar way? Or does his statement, "as to one untimely born", subtly acknowledge that it was of a different character from the others?[68]

When in Galatians 1:15–16, Paul refers to his "call" by God to evangelise the Gentiles, he speaks about God revealing Jesus to him in a manner that suggests a subjective experience, especially if we understand the Greek *en emoi* as "in me" rather than "to me".[69] Nonetheless, I would argue that Paul, certainly when he includes himself in the list of witnesses to the resurrection in 1 Corinthians 15, understands these appearances in a wholly objective fashion. To begin with, Paul first of all wants to establish in his readers' minds, or better remind them of, the tradition that Jesus was raised on the third day and appeared to a number of different individuals and groups. In the strangely circular nature of the argument that he then develops, it is not immediately clear why he would need to do this. After all, he then argues that Christ must have been raised, on the basis of the fact that there is a general resurrection of the dead (drawing on the ancient Jewish belief of a resurrection at the end of time). But, "if the dead are not raised, then Christ has not been raised" (v. 16). To be sure, he then reverses this to say that the resurrection of Christ is an earnest, if not a proof, of the fact that all will one day be raised from death. He also wishes to stress that Jesus's resurrection was a "bodily resurrection", even though he will then argue that a resurrection body is a different sort of body from one's pre-death physical body. In his view of resurrection as involving a resurrected body, Paul is simply showing his Jewish roots, for Jews could not conceive of a resurrection without a body.

Everywhere in the New Testament writings, both in Paul and in the writings of others, the resurrection of Jesus is presented as, and it is taken for granted that it is an objective occurrence, something God has done. According to Luke, Peter states it flatly on the day of Pentecost: "This Jesus God raised up, and of that all of us are witnesses" (Acts 2:32; cf. Acts 10:39–41; 13:28–31). Paul introduces his letter to the Romans with a summary of the "gospel concerning [God's] Son, who was descended from David according to the flesh and was declared to be Son of God with power according to the s/Spirit of holiness by resurrection from the dead, Jesus Christ our Lord..." (Rom. 1:3–4; cf. 4:24; 6:4, 9; 7:4; 8:11, 34; 10:9). Everywhere, the claim that God raised Jesus from the dead is stated in a matter-of-fact manner (see e.g. Gal. 1:1; Eph. 1:20; Col. 2:12; 1 Thess 1:10; Heb. 13:20; 1 Peter 1:3, 21).

Returning to the claim of Paul to be included among the witnesses to the resurrected Jesus, we may note these words of Richard Hays:

> By describing this appearance as 'last of all, [Paul] links it with the resurrection appearances to Jesus' original circle of followers and distinguishes it from all subsequent visions and from the personal experience of Christ that all believers possess through the Holy Spirit; he is claiming to have come face to face with Jesus the Messiah whom God had raised up.[70]

Therefore, logically, belief in the resurrection of Jesus must have been the catalyst for the continuation of the Jesus movement. In one way and another, this is the witness of the entire New Testament, and even if the writings of the New Testament, especially the gospels, were produced several decades after the crucifixion of Jesus, there is no viable explanation for why they would have been written without a group of people believing that Jesus was an important figure, whose life, teachings, and death had continuing significance. Only their strong belief that God had resurrected Jesus from death can explain the direction and the developments of their subsequent beliefs in him.

What I mean is this: it is difficult to imagine the New Testament material being what it is if the early church created the story. The representation of the preaching of the resurrection would surely break down, or be incoherent, if we imagine that the disciples created the story. Why, for instance, would they require stories about women going to find an empty tomb, if their initial understanding was that God had raised Jesus to the right hand of God? Did they not have concepts of the translation of a righteous man to God to hand? Would they necessarily require stories of an apparent bodily resurrection to make the point that Jesus was a special agent of God, a prophet, a Messiah even?

There is also the fact that the representation of Jesus is a remarkably coherent account of an incoherent idea. The claims made for Jesus that he is God incarnate or that through him God was working the salvation of humankind. Had these accounts be made up, even under the influence of beliefs and myths current at the time, would not the claims of the gospel writers fall apart under the weight of the preposterous claims being made? Too much time had elapsed, too many people would know a different story. There would be far more, far different accounts, produced.

Thus, the second approach is to try and grapple with the witness of the first Christians, and the written deposit of their beliefs as found in the New Testament. When they proclaimed that God has raised Jesus up what did they understand by this? What was the shape and character of their resurrection belief? What is the character of the event that seems to have been the catalyst for their continuing allegiance to, and proclamation of Jesus as Messiah and Lord? From whence did it arise, and how did it relate to the life and teachings, and the course of the ministry of the human person, Jesus, to whom they gave their allegiance, and to whom they applied their devotion?

CHAPTER THREE

A Sketch of the Historical Jesus

In the light of what has gone before, I now proceed to present my "sketch" of the historical Jesus's life, and death, to draw out his historical significance. This means that I shall provide what I think is a picture of Jesus that aims at a portrait of what is "characteristic" of the historical Jesus. This must be a story that sets him appropriately within his first-century Palestinian context, while also explaining how the memory of his life and death gave rise to the claims and beliefs of the early church. Most particularly is there a bridge (or are there bridges) that connect the pre-Easter Jesus with the post-Easter Jesus: and what might these be?[71]

I begin with the proposition that Jesus was seen as a prophet. I also think that Jesus saw himself as a prophet who stood within the tradition and line of the Old Testament prophets. John the Baptist also stood within this tradition and line, and demonstrated some of the concerns (for justice, and right living, for example) of the prophets. Jesus (and John the Baptist) came with the same intentions and objectives of many of the Old Testament prophets, namely, to recall the people of Israel to a true and proper understanding of what it meant to be the "covenant people"; what their calling to be the people of their God truly meant for individual and corporate life. Thus, when it came to the content of Jesus's teaching, there was both a reformative aspect, an aspect that called God's people to take up the inherent and fundamental purposes of the law (the true "fulfilling of the law", if you will), and an "eschatological" aspect: that is a pointing to the day when the purposes of God for Israelite society would be fully realised.

These two aspects (reformative and eschatological) make up the meaning and are the content of Jesus's proclamation of "the kingdom of God". There is a call to live as people who adhere to the values and ethos of the kingdom. This call is seen, for example, in the teaching that is found in the "Sermon on the Mount". In this call, Jesus insists that he is not overturning the law, but is calling for an adherence to the true essence of the law. God's will is to be done on earth, as it is in heaven. Even if Matthew added the line: "Your will be done on earth as it is in heaven" to the prayer as Jesus originally taught it (compare Matt. 6:10 with Luke 11:2b), I believe this clause well captures Jesus's intention.

As for the "eschatological" aspect, this was a reiteration in a new time of the Old Testament prophets' looking forward to the "Day of the Lord". This "day of the Lord" did not have a single meaning for the prophets. In some cases it referred to a time when God would act in judgment on the nation of Israel (see e.g. Amos 5:18–20; Micah 5:10–15; Zechariah 14:1–2); at other times it was a time of blessing, and God's salvation for Israel (see Amos 9:11–15; Micah 4:1–5; Zechariah 14:6–9). The central thing was that God would act to establish righteousness and justice: it would be a day when God's kingdom would come.

In Jesus's teaching, this naturally took on an apocalyptic hue as apocalypticism had become a feature in the literature and thinking of the post-prophetic Second Temple era. However, in Jesus's teaching, particularly in the apocalyptic material in the Synoptic Gospels, the contours and shape of this future when God would act decisively was left reasonably general and vague.

Jesus's understanding of the Kingdom of God and his prophetic role.

As Jesus saw himself as standing within the prophetic tradition of Israel, the tension often seen between the kingdom of God as the rule of God or the kingdom as a realm, as well as the tension between Jesus as an apocalyptic/eschatological prophet and a teacher of wisdom may be resolved.

At the heart of Jesus's mission and teaching was the understanding that not just the people of Israel, but all of humanity,[72] was called to live in a relationship with God, a relationship of trust, obedience, and of submission to the rule of God. In this sense, life in the kingdom of God was an extension of the covenant relationship that had been established with the people of Israel through the covenant first made with Abraham, and then extended through the covenant relationship established at Sinai, through Moses. As an aside, the understanding of the covenant as bringing Israel under the rule of God (God was their true king)[73] is perhaps why the concept of "the kingdom of God" as a realm is not found in the Old Testament. It was taken for granted that the land where God "planted" God's people (namely, what became known as ancient Palestine) was God's realm.[74]

What was most important, however, was the concept of "kingdom" as "God's rule", God's kingship. Hence the basic intention of Jesus's mission was to call people to take up, and to hold to, the "rule of God" in their lives. This had communal (or societal and political) implications as well. In this sense of calling people to recognise, acknowledge and respond to the reign and rule of God, Jesus was engaged in a "restoration" of Israel as well: the covenant relationship was to be renewed, a relationship that at heart acknowledged and lived under the reign/rule of God.

This reign/rule of God entailed an ethic, a way of life. Much of this was spelled out, for instance, in the Sermon on the Mount, which included the injunction to "be perfect...as your heavenly Father is perfect" (Matt. 5:48). This set the bar very high: and, note, this injunction to

God-like perfection (the Greek word could also mean to be "complete" or, we might say, "whole"), concluded a set of antitheses the last of which enjoined love for enemies. Those who persecute you are to be prayed for, so that you might be a child of your Father in heaven (5:43, 44), emulating God's attitude and behaviour in treating both righteous and unrighteous equally. And Jesus also commended as blessed those who were persecuted for *righteousness'* sake (5:10): it is they who would receive the kingdom.[75]

The rule of God required that people use their God-given capabilities well, and to bring a reward for God. Jesus told a parable of a nobleman (or master) giving his servants (slaves) varying degrees of responsibility (represented by differing amounts of money) and then holding them to account for how they had discharged their commission (see Matt. 25:14–30//Luke 19:11–27). There was an occasion when Jesus was asked his opinion on whether one should pay taxes to the emperor (or his local representative). Jesus asked to be shown a denarius, which bore an image of the emperor on it. When Jesus asked whose image was on the coin, and received the answer, "the emperor's", he said: "Give to the emperor the things that are the emperor's, and to God the things that are God's" (Mark 12:17//Matt. 22:21//Luke 20:25). This answer neatly placed the priorities where they should lie in the view of Jews who recognised the ultimate rule of God. They would realise that Jesus was alluding to the fact that humans were made in the image of God (Gen. 1:26), and so their very selves belonged to God. Nonetheless, under the political circumstances they found themselves in, taxes were due to the emperor and they should meet their obligation. However, Jesus left them to determine where their primary allegiance lay when God's will and the emperor's will should come into opposition.

The parable of the Good Samaritan addressed the question of how one should treat one's "neighbour" (a category neatly widened by Jesus when he made the Samaritan the one who helped the man in need). Anyone who wished to be a member of God's kingdom was to show mercy and compassion towards others. In fact, Luke when he provided the teaching on love of enemies (derived from the "Q" tradition) concluded the teaching by stating: "Be merciful, just as your Father is merciful" (Luke 6:36).

Matthew's gospel twice has Jesus citing Hosea 6:6; "For I desire steadfast love (or mercy) and not sacrifice." On the first occasion, Jesus is criticised for eating with tax collectors and sinners (Matt. 9:13). On the second occasion, the disciples had been plucking corn on the Sabbath, and Jesus was criticised, presumably for not stopping them (Matt 12:7). This time Jesus also refers to the incident in 1 Sam. 21:1–6, when David requisitioned the "the bread of the Presence" from the sanctuary at Nob, an expediency driven by hunger, but religiously unlawful. In Mark's version of this story, Jesus concludes with an aphorism, the first part of which is: "The sabbath was made for humankind, not humankind for the sabbath" (Mark 2:27). Soon after Mark records this incident, he recounts another in which Jesus heals a man with a withered hand on the sabbath. Sensing opposition from his opponents, Jesus asks "Is it lawful to do good or to do harm on the sabbath, to save life or to kill?" (Mark 3:4)

Jesus, it seems, took matters back to first principles in his teaching. What was the essence of God's will? As God's will was expressed through the law, was its intention to be life-giving or not? This going back to first principles is seen in his reply to a legal expert who asked him which commandment in the law was the greatest. In reply, Jesus quoted Deuteronomy 6:5: "You shall love the Lord your God with all your heart, and with all your soul, and with all your mind." But he immediately twins this with a second, drawn from Leviticus 19:18: "And a second is like it: 'You shall love your neighbour as yourself.'" And he concluded by saying that "[o]n these two commandments hang all the law and prophets." (Matt. 22:34–40). The fundamental bedrock of the law, then, is love for God and love for neighbour.

It is possible that in identifying love of God and love of neighbour as the heart of the law, and, if you will, its central intention, Jesus was highlighting an understanding of the law's intention that was shared by others among his Jewish contemporaries. At any rate, when Mark provides this story, he has Jesus quote the *Shema* in full: "Hear, O

Israel: the Lord our God, the Lord is one; you shall love the Lord your God with all your heart, and with all your soul, and with all your mind, and with all your strength." He then marries this with the injunction to love one's neighbour as oneself. This elicits a positive response from his interlocutor, whom Mark identifies as a scribe, who states that Jesus is correct to identify these as the most important commandments; and, the scribe concludes, "this is more important than all whole burnt offerings and sacrifices" (Mark 12: 28–34). Indeed, in Luke's version of this account, it is the "lawyer" who puts the two elements, love of God and love of neighbour, together (Luke 10:25–28), so Luke obviously understands that someone other than Jesus might make the connection between these commandments and identify them as the heart of the law.

It is interesting to note that in Mark, Jesus's response to the scribe's commendation, and reiteration of the point is to say that the scribe is "not far from the kingdom of God" (Mark 12:34). In Luke, this is captured in Jesus's return question to the lawyer's question about how he might "inherit eternal life": "What is written in the law? How do you read?" (i.e. how do you understand the law). The man's reply that love of God and love of neighbour go together (by implication, as the heart of the law), elicits Jesus's comment: "You have answered right; do this, and you will live." (Luke 10:25–28). We might note that the lawyer's further response in wanting to know whom he should consider a neighbour whom he should love, draws from Jesus the parable of the Good Samaritan. When asked which of the three men who came upon the man lying beside the road acted as a neighbour to him, the lawyer replies (somewhat reluctantly we might imagine): "The one who showed him mercy". To which Jesus said: "Go and do likewise." (Luke 10:37).

The point of this is that Matthew was quite right to have Jesus say, in the Sermon on the Mount, that he had not come to abolish the law or the prophets, but to fulfil (Matt 5:17). Jesus's intent was to get to the heart of what belonging to the kingdom of God was all about. In essence, to truly be law-abiding, to truly fulfil the law was to get to the heart of what God required which was absolute love and commitment to God, and a love of neighbour which resulted in compassionate action and just living. On one occasion, Jesus is portrayed as excoriating the scribes and Pharisees, for tithing mint, dill, and cumin while neglecting the "weightier matters of the law, justice and mercy and faith" (Matthew 23:23; Luke says they neglect, "justice and the love of God" [Luke 11:42]). This is not necessarily a matter of "either/or": rather it is a matter of "both/and"–"these [the weightier matters] you ought to have done, without neglecting the others."[76]

In his teaching that goes to the heart of the law, and beyond that to the central concern of what it means to be in a covenant relationship with God or, to put it in the terms Jesus used, to belong to the kingdom of God, Jesus stood firmly within the prophetic tradition. We might recall Micah 6:8: "He has told you, O mortal, what is good: and what does the Lord require of you but to do justice, and to love kindness and to walk humbly with your God?"[77] There are countless places in the prophetic literature where the prophet, speaking for God, condemns the people of Israel (or Judah) for betraying their calling as God's people (although outwardly perhaps, religious and "law-abiding") by acting unjustly, without mercy or compassion for the vulnerable. One text that captures the same type of juxtaposition between religious observance and the practice of justice and righteousness as found in Jesus's approach to the issue is Amos 5:21–24, where God is presented as objecting to the Israelite festivals, assemblies, sacrifices and songs, while calling for justice and righteousness (manifestly missing) to be done. Other texts that emphasise the need for justice may be found in Amos 8:4–6; Isa. 1:21–23, Isa 5:8–23[78]; Micah 2:1-2; 3:1–3; Habakkuk 2:6–17.

My point here, then, is that Jesus, like the prophets, was calling Israel back to its core covenant commitments. In this sense, Jesus was a "restoration prophet", or a prophet calling for the renewal of Israel.[79] His attacks on the Pharisees, scribes and religious leaders were over what he saw as their failure to uphold the justice and mercy that God required. Jesus did not necessarily oppose what they said (see Matt. 23:2), but condemned them for an outward show of religiosity that masked a neglect of justice, or, in some cases a perpetuation of injustice (Luke 20:45–47; 11:37–52; Matt 23:1–36): they "devour widows' houses", they build the prophets' tombs and supposedly revere them, but really stand in succession to the prophets' opponents and murderers.

The kingdom of God, then, was the rule of God in the lives of God's people. This would naturally have implications for the concept of the kingdom of God as a "realm", for the kingdom was to be embodied in human persons located in geographic places. But just as the prophetic tradition had a future aspect to it, namely, "the day of the Lord", when God would act in judgment and in salvation, so also Jesus's teaching of the kingdom had a future aspect.

The eschatological aspect of Jesus's teaching about the kingdom.

Amongst scholars who study the historical Jesus, a major area of debate is whether or not Jesus was an eschatological or apocalyptic prophet. That is, did or did Jesus not teach, and himself expect, the sudden and imminent action of God in the world to establish the kingdom? Was the reign of God, with its attendant judgment of the wicked and vindication of the righteous, just around the corner, as it were?

It is in considering this debate that it is helpful to keep in mind Jesus's sense, I argue, of standing in line with the prophets of old. For they too, in their teaching and preaching, held in tension a present need for Israel to return to its core covenant commitments, expressed especially in a pursuit of justice and mercy, and a future "day of the Lord" when God would establish "the kingdom". They, too, maintained a tension between blessing and judgment; and between present adherence of the covenant (often highlighting Israel's failure to do so) and the future restoration of "the remnant", and the reestablishment of God's people in a true covenant relationship with God, securely settled in their land. The "day of the Lord" in prophetic teaching taken as a whole was somewhat ambiguous. In some cases it referred to a day when Israel (or Judah) would suffer defeat at the hands of a foreign power, and so the nation would be punished (Isaiah 1: 7–9; 3: 16–4:1; Hosea 10; Zephaniah 1:2–13[80]; 3:14–20; Amos 2:4–16; 3:13–4:3; 5:1–20, 25–27; 6:11–14), or possibly judgment would come by a natural disaster (Joel

1:2–12; Amos 4:7–9). At other times, the day of the Lord is a day when God will act in judgment while the exact nature of the judgment is not specified (see Amos 5:16–20[81]).

On the other hand, "the day of the Lord" was a time when God would act to bless, restore and renew the fortunes of Israel (see Isa 2:2–4, cf. Mic 4:1-3[82]; Isa 4:2-6; 43:1–7; 44:1–5; 49:1–13; Isa 54-55; Hos 2:14–23; 14:4–7; Joel 2:18–29[83]; 3:18–21; Amos 9:11–15; Mic 2:12–13[84]; 7:11–20; Zech 14 [see especially vv 8, 9 and 21b]; Mal 4:1–3). In some cases the prophet announced this would be achieved through the operations of a special agent of God, who by the time of Jesus came to be known as "the Messiah"; or a descendant of David who would take up a righteous rule. Isaiah 7:14–15; 9:1–7; chapters 11 and 12; 42:1–9 all speak about this coming ruler in non-specific terms (a child, a "shoot from the stump of Jesse", viz. some Davidic ruler, although from 11:11 into chapter twelve the focus is on the Lord God, "the Holy One of Israel"), as do Amos 9:11 (again the restoration of a Davidic king), Zech 9:9–10 and Mic 5:2–5a (a ruler strongly associated with the Lord, and the words "whose origin is of old" suggests a divine personage, unless it means this ruler comes from an old and long dynasty). A couple of texts, Haggai 2:20–23, and Zech 6:9–15 are specifically (or appear to be) linked with a known descendant of David's, Zerubbabel (who became Governor of Judah after the exile).[85]

Malachi 3:1–4 and 4:5 speak of a messenger and the prophet Elijah as coming before the coming of the Lord (or in the case of Elijah "the great and terrible day of the Lord"). The gospel writers pick up this expectation of the messenger and Elijah and apply it to John the Baptist (see Mark 1:2[86]; 9:11–13). Mark 1:6//Matt 3:4 describe John the Baptist's dress in a way that is most probably intended to evoke that of Elijah. The implication is that, if John the Baptist is Elijah who was to precede the coming of the Lord, then the Lord that followed John the Baptist was Jesus (see Mark 1:2–8//Matt 3:3–4// cf. Matt 11:10; Luke 7:27). On one occasion, Jesus asks the disciples who people think he is, and they report that some believe Jesus to be (the returned) Elijah (see

Mark 8:28//Matt 16:14//Luke 9:19). Peter, however, identifies Jesus as the Messiah.

The gospel writers, in their presentations of Jesus, drew on many of the Old Testament prophetic passages about the coming king/messiah in showing the significance of Jesus. Matthew, for instance, in his story of the visit of the wise men has the chief priests quote Micah 5:2 as indicating where the Messiah is to be born. In Matt 12:17–21, the evangelist specifically draws upon the first of Isaiah's servant songs (Isa 42:1–4) in order the highlight the meaning of Jesus's ministry. The story of Jesus's entry into Jerusalem, seated on a donkey (conventionally called "the Triumphal Entry", see Mark 11:1–10//Matt 21:1–9//Luke 19:28–40//John 12:12–18) is told in such a way to evoke the prophecy in Zechariah 9:9, and, in fact, this text is specifically quoted in both Matthew's and John's accounts (see Matt 21:4,5; John 12:14-15).

Did Jesus himself, however, make statements or use scripture in ways that suggest he thought of himself as the coming Messianic agent? On two occasions in Luke's Gospel Jesus is represented as drawing upon Isaiah's prophecy (Isa 61:1–2a) of a figure who would bring good news and healing. The first is Jesus's sermon in the synagogue at Nazareth (Luke 4:16–30, see vv. 18, 19), and the second is when a delegation comes from John the Baptist inquiring whether or not Jesus is the expected messiah. In this second case, Jesus evokes the themes of Isaiah, rather than quoting directly (Luke 7:18–23//Matt 11:2–6).[87]

Following Jesus's protest action in the Temple (Mark 11:15–19//Matt 21:12–13//Luke 19:45–46), he is questioned about his authority for doing such an action. In reply Jesus tells a parable of some wicked tenants who refuse to give the owner his rightful share of the harvest. The tenants beat up and mistreat all the servants (slaves) that the owner sends. They even kill some he sends, and in the end, hoping that they will respect his son, he sends him. The tenants kill him and throw his body out of the vineyard (see Mark 12:1–12//Matt 21:33–46//Luke 20:9–19). In concluding his parable, Jesus quotes from Psalm 118:22–23 about the "chief cornerstone" rejected by builders. His opponents to whom this parable is told perceive that the parable is told against them, and would like to have arrested Jesus. It is obvious that Jesus applied this parable to himself: whether or not he intended to represent himself as "God's son" (at the heart of the issue of authority, was whether Jesus was acting on God's authority or not), the implication of the parable is that he regarded himself as in a special relationship to the prophets that came before him. Not only was he part of a long line of rejected prophets, but he was in some sense superior to them. This parable is one of the four "happy few" that John P. Meier considers to be an authentic parable from Jesus.[88]

The temple action, followed by the parable of the wicked tenants, leads into a series of questions put to Jesus by various groups and persons. These exchanges are concluded when Jesus asks his interlocutors (identified in Matthew as Pharisees, but in Mark and Luke this is more open[89]) how the Messiah can be called "the son of David", when David calls him "Lord" (citing Ps. 110:1); see Matt 22:41–46//Mark 12:35–37/Luke 20:41–44. What is the motivation for this exchange? What is Jesus's reason for asking this question? Or, perhaps more to the point, what are the evangelists suggesting by placing this exchange here? The exchange concludes a series of questions and tests of Jesus's authority, which began with the chief priests, scribes and elders asking Jesus on what authority he does "these things" (Mark 11:27–33//Matt 21:23–27//Luke 20:1–8). Jesus has countered with a question about whether John the Baptist's baptism, and by extension his authority for baptising, was from heaven (i.e. authorised by God) or "from men" (i.e. he undertook his baptising on his own initiative). The authorities refuse to answer, and so Jesus says he will not provide them with an answer for the source of his authority. The question is left hanging: Is Jesus a "prophet" as the ordinary people held John the Baptist to have been; and did, therefore, his authority come from God? And if Jesus's parable of the wicked tenants implies that he may have a status higher than other prophets what might that status be? The implication of Jesus's question about the Messiah is that this person, being David's "Lord" is indeed very high status indeed, a divine agent or possibly even God. A further implication is that if Jesus is operating by divine authority, then possibly he operates with the authority of the Messiah, the "Son of David", the expected descendant of David who would bring renewal and peace to Israel.

How much of this derives from the evangelists' clever arrangement of "Jesus traditions", and use of scripture; and how much derives from Jesus's own self-understanding? My position is that the evangelists were reflecting an understanding of Jesus that they gained from Jesus's own understanding of his mission. This is confirmed, I will argue below, from a particular way Jesus had of referring to himself as "the Son of Man". It is also seen in his teaching with authority, and in a couple of prophetic actions: his entry into Jerusalem on a donkey, and his protest action in the Temple (which sparked the questions about his authority).

An "apocalyptic" prophet?

In the previous section, I have endeavoured to show how Jesus can be seen to stand within the prophetic tradition, which had both a "present" aspect in that the prophets addressed the sins and situation of the nation at the time of their prophesying, and also a future dimension that looked forward to a "day of the Lord" when God would act decisively in judgment and redemption. However, in the first century the expectation of God's action had acquired an apocalyptic cast, so that "the day of the Lord" became a future age, when God's intervention would bring to an end the "present age". There arose a sharp disjunction between "the present age" (which lay under the rule of God's Adversary) and the "age to come", where God would reign supreme. Jesus shared this kind of outlook, though his focus was generally on the coming of the kingdom, and, in particular, he associated this future event with the coming of the Son of Man (with whom he associated himself; see e.g. Mark 8:38).[90]

Jesus's teaching had to do with being ready for God's coming kingdom which one did by being faithful in living as God required. The servant who got about his master's business, and undertook his responsibilities faithfully and well, was the one who was ready for the master's coming (whenever that was). Jesus's apocalyptic language was down-to-earth, and "matter-of-fact" as compared with the type of apocalyptic found elsewhere.

Was Jesus an apocalyptic or a non-apocalyptic prophet? My answer is that this is not an "either/or" matter: he combined elements of both. He was immersed in a society where "apocalyptic type" thinking was in the air, and he both imbibed this and drew on it to get his message across. But Jesus was more concerned with the reign of God, than with when and how it would happen; or to put it in other words, Jesus attention was focused upon establishing the reign of God, and bringing Israel under the conditions of that kingdom, not upon the end of time. There are some indications that Jesus may have thought that the time when the kingdom would be fully present, was near. On the other hand, he believed that only "the Father" knew the time of its occurrence. What Jesus did know was that he had a role to play in it as the Son of Man.

Jesus as a teacher who taught in parables.

A remembered and memorable aspect of Jesus's teaching was the way in which he used parables. These short, pointed and metaphorical or similitude stories were a feature of Jesus's teaching method. Here I must raise an objection, and point out an inconsistency (as I see it) in the approach of John P. Meier to the parables. The problem with his approach is a direct result of his dependence upon the criteria of authenticity. He is able to identify only four parables as certainly authentic to Jesus. These are the parables of the mustard seed (Mark 4:30–32//Matt 13:31–32//Luke 13:18–19); "the evil tenants of the vineyard" (Mark 12:1–11; Matt 21:33–43; Luke 20:9–18); "the great supper" (Matt 22:2–14; Luke 14:16–24); and the parable of "the talents/pounds" (Matt 25:14–30//Luke 19:11–27). Nonetheless, Meier considers the fact that Jesus told parables a secure historical fact: a conclusion supported by the multiply attested nature of the phenomenon.[91] On many of the parables, Meier returns a verdict of *"non liquet"*, that is, the matter cannot be decided for or against whether Jesus told the particular parable. My question is this: if the historical Jesus was a teller of parables, why not assume that any parable that is "undecided", must have come from the historical Jesus?[92]

There is a further reason to take this course. If Jesus told memorable parables, as many of the parables are, why should we assume that the disciples would not be able to remember them? Furthermore, if Jesus did not tell the parable of the Good Samaritan, or the Prodigal Son, to choose two of the most well-known and well-loved parables, who did? I do not believe these were created by an anonymous group of believers. Meier would attribute the parable of the Good Samaritan to Luke.[93] I would concur: if Jesus is not the original teller of the parable, then Luke is as good a choice as any, and probably the best choice. But in that case, why not focus on Luke as a superb creator (and "teller"?) of parables? Why, indeed, does "Luke" attribute the parables to Jesus? And how is it possible that no early Christian tradition identified Luke as the creative genius who was a superb creator of parables?

One of the implications of the tendency of scholars to slough off Jesus tradition onto the early church is that, contrary to normal human behaviour, we must assume that everyone in the early church seems to have entered into a "conspiracy of silence" over the origins of the material. All was attributed to Jesus; no one let slip that, actually, Luke (for instance) created that story–unless, of course, we should understand Papias's testimony as meaning that when he enquired from followers of "the elders" what Andrew, Peter, Philip, Thomas, James, John or Matthew, or any other of the Lord's disciples said, he was also identifying the actual authors of (not tradents or witnesses to) Jesus material. I do not deny that tradents, or in the case of the gospels the evangelists, played a part in shaping the material that was handed down. The evangelists, for instance, manifestly arrange and order, and in many cases, craft the wording (they had to as they were providing a translation into Greek of Jesus's words) of Jesus's teaching. But that is a different exercise from the creation of a Jesus tradition out of "whole cloth" as it were. My objection to some of the approach of scholarship is that it does not seem to ask questions about the sociological or human implications of, as it seems to me, often blithely attributing material to the creative activity of the first followers of Jesus.[94]

Let us assume, then, that the parabolic material we find in the Synoptic Gospels comes substantially from the historical Jesus. What does this tell us about the teaching style of Jesus? For one thing, it was memorable. For another, it seems that Jesus often left his hearers to draw their own conclusions: or rather, to figure out for themselves the meaning and the implication of the story. Sometimes that was relatively straightforward. The parable of the Good Samaritan is followed by Jesus asking his interlocutor which of the men acted as neighbour. The lawyer was quite easily able to identify the Samaritan as the one, for he had shown "mercy". Jesus simply said: "Go and do likewise." On another occasion, he told the religious authorities a story about a man who had a vineyard which was let out to tenants, who refused to give the owner his due, and in fact mistreated and/or killed the owner's agents, including the most important agent, his son. The religious authorities had no difficulty in identifying whom the tenants represented: and they resented Jesus telling the story.

At other times, the parable Jesus told was somewhat ambiguous. On one occasion, after Jesus had told a parable about a sower sowing seeds, Mark has the disciples coming to Jesus to ask for an explanation of the parable (see Mark 4:1–20). Jesus explains the parable as having to do with how one should attend to "the word", by extension, how one should take care to listen to his teaching. This is a perfectly understandable explanation, and makes good sense of the parable. However, taken by itself without the explanation, one might take the meaning of the parable to do with the kingdom and the way the kingdom progresses or not in various circumstances (there are other parables that apply concepts of growth to the kingdom).[95]

Indeed, the two parables that follow the parable of the sower in Mark's Gospel are both relatively ambiguous. What does the parable of the growing seed (Mark 4:26–29) mean? That the kingdom of God grows inevitably and surely, without any obvious outside agency, but, like the earth producing grain "of itself"? Or does it mean that "a harvest" (the arrival of the kingdom?) is sure to come? In the parable of the mustard seed: who or what are "the birds" that make nests in the large branches of the grown shrub/tree? Is this simply an incidental detail emphasising the size of the tree? Or should we understand this to mean that all manner of people find "shelter" in the kingdom of God, or does it refer specifically to Gentiles?

Whether the parables Jesus told were relatively straightforward, or designed to tease the mind into active thought,[96] they covered a range of topics. Quite a number of the narrative parables had to do with judgment, and being ready for the coming of the kingdom, or the king/messiah (pictured as the arrival of a bridegroom in one parable). Others had to do with how one used one's time, or capabilities.

The term "parable" could cover more than just narrative parables. We find in the gospels that Jesus was also the master of the aphorism, the maxim, the riddling or enigmatic statement, the proverb and the wise saying. So we have, for instance, Jesus saying such things as "The sabbath was made for humankind, not humankind for the sabbath" (Mark 2:27), or "You are the light of the world. A city built on a hill cannot be hid" (Matt 5:14), or "Wisdom is vindicated by all her children" (Luke 7:35). Jesus, then, told memorable stories, and spoke in pithy ways that were memorable.

Jesus's non-parabolic teaching.

Much of Jesus's teaching, particularly in Matthew's Gospel where there are five great "blocks of teaching" is not parabolic, although the Beatitudes, with which the first great (and longest) block of teaching begins, are aphoristic in style. Another type of teaching saw Jesus provide a series of antitheses which deepened or widened the scope of traditional Torah instruction. On other occasions, Jesus gave what might be taken as wise advice, or "common sense" instructions: e.g. if you go to a wedding banquet, seat yourself where you will be likely to be promoted to a better seat rather than asked to move for someone more important than yourself (Luke 14:7–11)

I don't intend to be comprehensive, but merely to make the point that in his teaching Jesus used a variety of methods, and styles. In particular, he was known for teaching "with authority"; and in a manner different from the scribes or other rabbis of the time. His teaching had a kind of sovereign authority to it that was not only authoritative but gave him status as a teacher (rabbi) in people's eyes.

Jesus as Exorcist and Healer.

That Jesus was an exorcist is one of the more widely agreed upon aspects of Jesus's ministry. For one thing, it is recognised that exorcism was an activity carried on by others as well as Jesus. This is attested within the New Testament (see e.g. Matt 12: 27//Luke 11:19; Acts 19:13–16). Geza Vermes sees Jesus as part of "charismatic Judaism", and places Jesus alongside other Jewish exorcists and healers.[97] It is certainly the case that Jesus's healing ministry was something that the gospel writers saw as undergirding his claim to be a prophet, and in their eyes the Messiah (see Matt 11:4, 5//Luke 7:22) and Jesus is represented as stating that his power to perform exorcisms is a sign that God's kingdom has arrived (Luke 11:20). In his healing activity Jesus stood in the line of Elijah and Elisha.

Jesus as a doer of miracles.

The miracles that Jesus is reported to have done in the gospels pose one of the more difficult aspects of Jesus's ministry to assess.[98] If the historical Jesus (or, as I would argue, the historical Christ) can perform a miracle like the feeding of the five thousand (a miracle that I think did occur), then surely he can also walk on water.

However, I think that in the case of walking on water, there are quite a few variations, and puzzles in the stories, to suggest that possibly the theological points being made predominate over the facticity of the occurrence of water-walking. To begin with, there is an interesting distinction to be drawn between the account in John's Gospel and those in the Synoptic Gospels. For one thing, in John's Gospel, the Greek construction leaves open the question of whether Jesus was walking on the water, or on the lake's shore. The Greek phrase is *epi tēs thalassēs*, translated "on the sea" (John 6:19), and it is this same phrase that is used in John 21:1 where it manifestly means "by [or beside] the sea of Tiberias".[99] Furthermore, the narrative proceeds in an interesting way: it states that the disciples "wanted to take [Jesus] into the boat, and immediately the boat reached the land toward which they were going." It is as if, moving to pick Jesus up, they find themselves at the shore and, indeed, the place that they were heading for.

When we look at the account in Matthew and Mark (Matt 14:22–33; Mark 6:45–52), we have further reason to think that theological themes are being brought to the stories. In Mark's Gospel, the narrator tells us that Jesus intended to pass them by, but when they cry out in fear, he says, "Take heart, *it is I*, do not be afraid." This is possibly to evoke the theme of a epiphany, and may bring to mind God "passing by" Moses in Exod 33:19–23; 34:6, and Elijah (1 Kgs 19:11).[100] Certainly, the words, "it is I" (italicised above), which in Greek are *egō eimi* echo God's self-identifying "I am" spoken to Moses in the story of the burning bush (Exod 3:14 LXX). So a theme of Jesus revealing himself in an epiphany to his disciples may be in play here. In Matthew's Gospel we have a theme of trusting in Jesus in the face of danger or challenge, as Peter is depicted as attempting to walk to Jesus on the water and needing to be rescued when he loses confidence in the face of the waves (see Matt 14:28–31). The same "I am" statement appears in the story (14:27) but Matthew goes one step further in having the disciples worship Jesus once he is in the boat, saying "Truly you are the Son of God" (14:33).

This shows that theological motivations may be affecting the telling of at least some of the miracle stories. We could find more: for example, eucharistic themes in the feeding stories (especially in Mark, which may influence John's use of the miracle, which is followed by a discourse on "the bread of life").[101] A further example is the way in which Mark presents a healing of a blind man which, unusually, requires two attempts at healing by Jesus (Mark 8:22–26). This perhaps represents the disciples' level of understanding of who Jesus is, and what his being the Messiah means, at this point in the story. Later Mark gives us the story of the healing of blind Bartimaeus (Mark 10:46-52), which forms an inclusio with the story in Mark 8:22–26. Bartimaeus represents one who sees clearly and follows Jesus "on the way". These two stories bracket a series of occasions on which Jesus teaches the disciples about his coming death, and what it means to be a disciple. The two stories of the blind men act as representations of different levels of understanding of this teaching.[102]

These examples indicate that the miracle stories that the evangelists relate, as with other elements of their gospels, are not necessarily straight accounts of how things happened. They have been put to the purpose of bringing out the true significance of Jesus, and his ministry, and the implications of this for the lives of hearers (or readers) of their gospels. This, however, does not obviate their use as sources of historical data. Historical Jesus scholars will come to different conclusions about the historicity of this or that miracle story (or elements within a story), but one may still be able to come to the conclusion that performing miracles, as with exorcisms, was a feature of the historical Jesus's ministry.[103]

The Jewish historian, Josephus, describes Jesus as a "doer of wonderful works" (*Ant.* 18.3.3 #63).[104] The Synoptic Gospels recognise, however, that exorcisms and miracles are not a sufficient indicator of who Jesus is. Exorcisms are considered by Jesus's opponents, or sceptics (see Luke 11:15), to mean that he is working under the influence of Beelzebul (Mark 3:22//Matt12:24//Luke 11:15). Jesus himself refuses to provide signs as a way of confirming his authority (see Mark 8:11, 12). In Matthew, Jesus meets the request of scribes and Pharisees for a sign, with a refusal but with an enigmatic reference to the sign of Jonah (a reference to his death): Jesus then makes statements that suggest that he is someone greater than both Jonah and Solomon (Matt 12:38–42, cf. Luke 11:29–32, where it is the crowds who receive Jesus's rebuke). Even in John's Gospel, where Jesus's miraculous deeds are identified as signs of Jesus's messiahship, the evangelist recognises that signs, and the reception of signs by onlookers, is no guarantee of true belief in Jesus. In John 2:23–25, the narrator states that many believed in Jesus on account of the signs (presumably miraculous deeds) that he was doing, but Jesus did not trust their response. In John 4:46–54, when a royal official asks Jesus to come and heal his son, Jesus replies, "Unless you (pl.) see signs and wonders you will not believe." This is an indication that the doing of signs and wonders is not sufficient to establish Jesus's identity, or to persuade people to truly believe in him.

Two prophetic acts.

All four gospels record two actions of Jesus which may be taken as symbolic and prophetic acts. They are enacted "signs" (to use the Johannine description) of Jesus's identity, and of his pronouncement of the coming kingdom. These are the "triumphal" entry of Jesus into Jerusalem riding on a donkey (Mark 11:1–11; Matt 21:1–16; Luke 19:28–40; John 12:12–19), and the "cleansing" of (or Jesus's dramatic action in) the Temple (Mark 11:15–19; Matt 21:12–17; Luke 19:45–48; John 2:13–22). Both these incidents provide puzzles and conundrums for the scholar researching the life of the historical Jesus. We will look at each separately.

1. The triumphal entry into Jerusalem.

Some scholars raise questions about the historicity of this incident. The fact that it seems to deliberately echo the prophecy of Zechariah 9:9 suggests a story created to "fulfil" that text. Bultmann, who considers that Jesus intended to fulfil the prophecy, and that the crowds would have recognised the donkey as "the Messiah's beast of burden" as absurd, neatly puts the objection: "There can only be one question. Was the Entry as such historical, but made a Messianic one by legend, or has it developed completely out of the prophecy?"[105]

It is interesting to note that John's Gospel specifically identifies this incident (and the "cleansing" of the Temple, as it happens) as one where the disciples come to a fuller understanding of the event after the resurrection, and on the basis of the recollection of scripture (see John 12:16). Nonetheless, there is no inherent reason why this incident should not be taken as an action undertaken by Jesus. How it unfolded is not entirely clear. The Gospel of John almost suggests that Jesus mounted the donkey in response to the fact that he was met by crowds proclaiming the arrival of "the King of Israel". The other gospels that Jesus staged this act, perhaps to evoke the Zechariah prophecy, and Luke's Gospel indicates that it was the disciple band (described as a "multitude") that initiated the praise of Jesus.

Brent Kinman argues that the "triumphal" entry is historically plausible, and probable for a number of reasons. He sees this as an incident iniated by Jesus, who "intended to present himself as Israel's king and as a central eschatological figure of promise when he came to [Jerusalem] at the Passover season."[106] This would explain, also, why Jesus attracted a charge of claiming a kingship for himself, a charge that brought him to trial before Pilate and eventual crucifixion.

1. The "cleansing" of the Temple.

The "cleansing" of the Temple (to give it its conventional name within Christian tradition) was rather an act of political protest. The Synoptic Gospels place this incident immediately after Jesus's "triumphal" entry into Jerusalem. John's Gospel, however, separates it from the incident of the "triumphal" entry, and appears to place it at the time of Passover, two years prior to that incident.[107] This presents the historian with a conundrum: which is correct?

There is an interesting harmonisation between the Synoptic accounts and the Johannine account that occurs when scholars place these incidents chronologically into an account of Jesus's ministry. Much of the time it is done unconsciously. Scholars tend to accept the Synoptic order of the "triumphal" entry to Jerusalem, placed just before the "cleansing" of the Temple. But they place the "triumphal" entry at the outset of the last week of Jesus's life. Now, the only way they can arrive at that is by taking the time reference provided in John's Gospel that it was "six days before the Passover" that Jesus came to Bethany, and the next day proceeded to Jerusalem (John 12:1, 12). Nowhere prior to the event do the Synoptic Gospels give a precise time for the entry into Jerusalem. In Mark's Gospel, we do not get a precise date until Mark 14:1, when we are told that it is "two days before the Passover". Prior to that we have a series of statements of a general nature, such as "on the following day" (11:12), "in the morning" (11:20). There is nothing to suggest when Jesus sets out for Jerusalem (a first reference to heading to Jerusalem appears in 10:32). This may have been three weeks prior to Jesus's death, or several more weeks prior, or only a few days prior. We do not know: but when Jesus is arrested in Gethsemane, he challenges the arresting party with this statement: "Have you come out with swords and clubs to arrest me as though I were a bandit? *Day after day* I was with you in the temple teaching, and you did not arrest me" (Mark 14:48, 49a). "Day after day": how long was that–three or four days, or several weeks? Neither Matthew nor Luke, who basically follow Mark in providing a precise time reference "two days" prior to Passover (Matt 26:2//Luke 26:2), provide any further clarification.[108]

Hence, what happens when scholars place the "triumphal" entry at the outset of the last week of Jesus's life, is that they take the time reference in John 12:1, and apply it to the Synoptic accounts as well. Although I called this a case of "harmonisation", this should not be taken in a pejorative sense. I mention this tendency to illustrate that a historical reconstruction of Jesus's life is something done by the historical scholar, out of and alongside of the gospel accounts. This type of harmonisation is perfectly legitimate, and is the normal activity undertaken by historians as they attempt to reconstruct historical events from diverse sources of data. The harmonisation that is more suspect, I suggest, is the proposal sometimes made in the case of the "cleansing" of the Temple, where in order to maintain the "historicity" of both the Synoptic and Johannine accounts, it is stated that Jesus performed this action twice. This seems to me to be unlikely: the accounts in the gospels give every indication of recounting the one (and same) event despite the differences in the details.

In terms of which of the chronological placements is correct, that is, historically accurate in terms of either placing this event early in Jesus's ministry (John's Gospel), or late, and perhaps, at a relatively short period before Jesus's arrest (Synoptic Gospels), a case could be made for either.[109] In the case of John's Gospel, one might argue that Jesus did this action, and it was a relatively small and contained protest (so did not attract attention from the Roman authorities) early on in his ministry. This propelled him sufficiently into public notice to put him on the map as it were (and begin to raise the interest and concern of the Jewish religious leaders). It would then account for his early success in attracting favourable notice among the people. It is sometimes said that the Temple action must have happened late, as it was one of the factors that lead to Jesus's arrest. However, a careful reading of the Synoptic Gospels shows that even the Jewish temple and religious authorities did not act immediately (although it is said that some of their caution was due to the popularity of Jesus among the people). Still, each Synoptic Gospel suggests that Jesus was able to leave the city that evening and return to Bethany, and it was not until the next day that any real challenge and questions about why he thought he had the authority to do the action arose (see Matt 21:17, 23//Mark 11: 19, 27–28//Luke 19:47; 20:1). In fact, each of the Synoptic Gospels has Jesus teaching in the temple after the incident. Luke is particularly vague about when Jesus was challenged. After the incident in the temple (an extremely brief account), he states that "every day [Jesus] was teaching in the temple" and it is only "one day" that he is challenged by the authorities. Matthew has Jesus healing in the temple after his protest action, and the authorities reacting angrily, but more over his healing activity and the fact that children were crying out "Hosanna to the Son of David" (Matt 21:14, 15), a cry that the children perhaps picked up from others during the "triumphal" entry. They challenge Jesus the following day: does the "these things" refer to the temple action, or the healing activity, or perhaps both? At any rate, there is no attempt made to arrest Jesus until after he has told some pointed parables against them (but they were afraid to do so, because "the crowds" regarded Jesus as a prophet, see Matt 21:46).

Many scholars prefer the Synoptic chronology.[110] Jesus's protest in the temple took place towards the end of his ministry, and shortly before his arrest. It is certainly the case that, according to their presentations, the opposition to Jesus began to really build into a definite desire on the part of the authorities to be rid of Jesus. When Jesus is arrested and interrogated by the Jewish religious leaders, the issue of his attitude to the temple comes up. Various witnesses, identified by the evangelists as "false witnesses", accuse Jesus as making threats against the temple.

Interestingly, it is in the account in John's Gospel that Jesus makes a statement that conceivably could have supplied the witnesses with their accusation. In John 2:19, when asked for a "sign" to establish his authority for his action, Jesus says, "Destroy this temple, and in three days I will raise it up." It is interesting to note that Matthew's and Mark's accounts give the impression that little headway is made in finding justification for condemning Jesus, until witnesses are found that accuse Jesus of speaking against the temple. Matthew's account states: "At last two [false witnesses] came forward and said, 'This fellow said, "I am able to destroy the temple of God and to build it in three days"'" (Matt 26:60b–61). Mark's Gospel has this: "Some stood up and gave false testimony against him, saying, 'We heard him say, "I will destroy this temple that is made with hands, and in three days I will build another not made with hands."' But even on this point their testimony did not agree" (Mark 14:57–59). The variations in the accounts suggests that Jesus's statement (which may be reasonably faithfully recorded in John's Gospel) was sufficiently ambiguous to give rise to disagreements amongst the witnesses as to what exactly he said. Significantly, Mark's version suggests that John's interpretation, that Jesus meant a metaphorical allusion to the temple of his body (John 2:21), may have been a possible construction to put upon his claim. The fact that this saying, however it was originally said, appears in the account of Jesus's interrogation before the Jewish leadership, implies that it is entirely plausible that Jesus made such a statement: and the version found in John may be close to the original.

Let us assume that the Synoptic chronology provides the best historical data regarding the placement of the temple action. I note in passing that the account in John's Gospel also ties the temple incident with Jesus's death (both in the metaphorical implication behind Jesus's enigmatic statement about the temple's destruction, and in the narrator's comment about the disciples retrospective remembrance after Jesus's resurrection *from the dead*.) What does this event signify? What is its meaning and import for understanding the historical Jesus?

Many scholars think that Jesus here is enacting a prophetic gesture signalling the temple's destruction. It is the action of an eschatological prophet envisaging the end of the temple, if not the end of the age.[111] It is certainly the case that Jesus is represented in the Synoptic Gospels as predicting the end of the temple (see Mark 13:2//Matt 24:2//Luke 21:5, 6; cf. Mark 13:14–an enigmatic statement, possibly linked to the fate of the temple).

I am inclined to think that Jesus's temple action was a protest against the activities going on in the temple court: the buying and selling of animals for sacrifice, the changing of money. It is possible that he considered the merchants selling animals were making an undue profit, and that the poor were especially hard done by; possibly also the money-changers were charging an unfair rate of exchange. This is borne out by the use of scripture wherein Jesus (citing Jeremiah 7:11) accuses the traders of turning the temple area into "a den of robbers" (Mark 11:17//Matt 21:13//Luke 19:46). In John's Gospel, Jesus accuses the traders of making the temple ("my Father's house") an emporium ("a house of trade"). In Mark's Gospel, Jesus not only interrupts the trade by driving out animals, and overturning the tables of moneychangers, but he also forbids anyone to make the temple a thoroughfare for carrying goods (perhaps items to be bought or sold).

It is, however, the first part of Jesus's statement, in which he quotes Isaiah 56:7 that is important for understanding his motivation. "My house shall be called a house of prayer for all the nations". The trading, and the general to-ing and fro-ing, would most likely be taking place in the "Court of the Gentiles", that area of the temple where Gentiles were permitted to come and worship. Their ability to worship and pray was probably severely hampered and disrupted by the noise, the bustle, and the commerce (which may have included a good amount of haggling) that was going on. While there is only a small amount of evidence that Jesus had interactions with non-Jews in his ministry, and, indeed, saw his ministry either solely or largely directed at his fellow Jews[112], he no doubt shared the prophetic vision of Israel as a "light to the nations". He would have concurred with the Isaianic prophecies (among others) of non-Jews coming to worship in the temple in Jerusalem.[113]

John's Gospel represents the disciples as recalling the scripture: "Zeal for your house will consume me" (Ps. 69:9; LXX). Whether or not, they would also have recalled other scriptures, such as Zechariah 14:21b, "...there shall no more be traders (or Canaanites, i.e. those "morally or spiritually unclean") in the house of the Lord of hosts on that day"; or Malachi 3:1, "...the Lord whom you seek will suddenly come to his temple", it is certain that the evangelist saw this action not only as a prophetic act, but as an act of the promised Messiah, whom his gospel was designed to show Jesus to be.[114] We might note, in passing, that the verb "will consume" may be taken as a veiled reference to Jesus's death: that is, Jesus is not only consumed with zeal for the proper use of the temple for worship, but his action in the temple contributes to the causes of his death.[115]

However the temple action is to be understood: as a symbolic prophecy of the temple's destruction, or as a prophetic protest against the commercial activities taking place within the temple precincts, both this action and the "triumphal" entry into Jerusalem are acts undertaken as prophetic actions like those of the Old Testament prophets. The gospel writers presented them as indications (or as "signs" to use John's Gospel terminology) of the fact that Jesus was the promised Messiah. What indications are there that Jesus himself saw himself as more than a prophet: as someone who came as God's special agent, and in a particular relationship to God?

CHAPTER FOUR

The Jesus of Faith and the Christ of History

There is little doubt that a shift of perspective took place in how Jesus was perceived and proclaimed after his death. Bultmann has neatly captured the essence of this shift in his statement that the Proclaimer became the Proclaimed.[116] In other words, Jesus whose message was the kingdom of God, and of which Jesus was the prophet calling people back to their covenant calling as God's people, and preparing them for the imminent arrival of that kingdom, became, in the proclamation of the early church, the expected Messiah. The early church's focus was upon Jesus as the Christ, whom God had designated "both Lord and Messiah" by the act of raising him from the dead (see Acts 2:32–36; Romans 1:4). Indeed, the first Christians were very quickly assigning Jesus a divine status alongside God, and calling Jesus "the Son of God".

For more than two hundred years, scholars have been trying to tease out the relationship between the Jesus who lived and died and the Jesus Christ whom the first Christians proclaimed after the resurrection. Indeed, we might better say that many scholars have been trying to separate out the Jesus of history from the Christ of faith, that is, the Jesus in whom the first Christians believed, and whom they proclaimed as the Christ, and Son of God.

But is there an essential continuity between the Jesus whom the first disciples knew as a historical human being before his crucifixion, and the Jesus whom they proclaimed as Christ and Lord after the (claimed) resurrection? And further to that, is their representation of the historical Jesus as the Christ, and as one proclaimed as Lord and God in their preaching, and in the New Testament gospels, a true representation of the historic significance of the historical person? In other words: may we also say that the historical Jesus is indeed the historical Christ? And in what way can we make that connection: as historians or only as believers? I shall return to this question below.

But first, to the matter of the essential continuity between how Jesus understood himself and as the early Christians proclaimed him. Is there a "bridge" between the two eras, if you will, that of the "pre-Easter Jesus" and that of the "post-Easter Jesus"? I would argue that there are three indicators of the essential continuity between pre-Easter and post-Easter Jesus. These are: the practice of the Lord's Supper by the early church; the use of the title "Son of Man" in the gospels; and the choice of an inner core of disciples called "the Twelve". Each of these are in themselves highly debated and complex issues, but I shall briefly outline them here and state why I think that these indicate that Jesus made claims and did things that prompted the first Christians to make the claims for him that they did.

The Lord's Supper (also known as the Holy Communion or Eucharist).

In Paul's first letter to the Corinthians, he refers to a couple of traditions that he has received. One, in 1 Corinthians 15:3–7, is a tradition that contains a list of the witnesses to the resurrection of Jesus.[117] The other tradition is found in 1 Corinthians 11:23–25 and relates to the institution of the Lord's Supper, also recorded in the Synoptic Gospels. In each case, Paul describes the tradition as something he received and handed on. It is true that, in the case of the tradition about the Lord's Supper, Paul says that he received it "from the Lord" (which might suggest a direct revelation), but the details and the wording are sufficiently like the traditions found in the Synoptic Gospels that one senses that Paul is referring to a tradition from Christian sources.[118] And the terms "received" and "handed on" are widely understood to be technical terms for the transmission of tradition.

It seems that from very early on (and in my opinion, likely shortly after the crucifixion and proclaimed resurrection of Jesus) the first Christians were meeting and having a meal with the symbolic breaking of bread and drinking of wine in remembrance of Jesus's death. They did this, so the tradition maintained, because Jesus himself on the night of his arrest had enacted this symbolic action and instructed that it be done "in remembrance of me" (so Luke 22:19 with reference to eating the bread, 1 Cor. 11:24, 25, with reference to both the bread and the wine).

It is, in fact, Paul's reference to a tradition he has received and passed on about what Jesus did on the night before he was betrayed, that indicates the practice was early. In 1 Corinthians 11: 23–25 (NRSV), he writes:

> For I received from the Lord what I handed on to you, that the Lord Jesus on the night when he was betrayed took a loaf of bread, and when he had given thanks, he broke it and said, "This is my body that is for you. Do this in remembrance of me." In the same way he took the cup also, after supper, saying, "This cup is the new covenant in my blood. Do this as often as you drink it, in remembrance of me."

His words of introduction, "For I received from the Lord what I handed on to you", indicate that he is drawing upon a tradition. Interestingly, this same kind of wording (indicating a tradition received and passed on) is used in 1 Corinthians 15:3a. Though Paul says that he received it from the Lord, it does not mean that he received it directly from the Lord, but rather that he wishes to stress that this is a genuine Jesus tradition. 1 Corinthians is thought by scholars to have been written in the early 50s CE,[119] less than twenty-five years after Jesus's crucifixion, and when Lord's Supper, according to the Synoptic Gospel accounts, was instituted. Noting that what Paul says here seems to suggest that this celebration of the Lord's Supper, or remembrance of Jesus's death, took place within the context of a meal (see 1 Corinthians 11:20–34),[120] we might surmise that references to "[breaking] bread at home" (Acts 2:46, "from house to house" according to a marginal reading) could well have included celebrating the Lord's Supper, suggesting that the early Christians carried this over from the initial institution by Jesus a few weeks earlier.

Despite the differences in wording amongst the traditions, the core of the tradition is clear. Jesus, gathered with his disciples for a meal, takes a piece of bread and says, "Take, this is my body" and then a cup of wine, saying, "This is my blood of the covenant that is poured out for many."[121] It is most probable that the bread was distributed amongst the disciples and they ate; and that the cup was passed around and the disciples all drank from it. Nicholas Perrin suggests that Jesus "intentionally laid hold of the *aphikomen*, the piece of bread traditionally set aside for the expected messiah and later identified with the messiah." He says that the evangelists "understood and sought to preserve this symbolism", so that the accounts depict Jesus as offering himself as the messiah and the disciples, by eating the bread, confess him as such.[122]

The nature of the tradition is such that it is most likely that it goes back to an actual event prior to the death of Jesus. The core of the event, and the words (or the intent of the words) are those expressed by Jesus at the time.[123] No doubt it was later remembered, and enacted differently on different occasions. But it is difficult to believe that the early Jewish believers would have invented such a tradition unless it had historical roots in the life of Jesus. Without the event of the resurrection, of course, no such tradition would exist.

The tradition of the Lord's Supper indicates, I argue, that Jesus understood his death to have a salvific significance for others. He saw himself as holding a special position within the purposes of Israel's God in establishing the kingdom. What Jesus understood by saying that the wine represented his blood "of the covenant" (or, "new covenant", so Luke and Paul), poured out for many, and, according to Matthew, "for the forgiveness of sins", is difficult to determine. The gospel writers represent Jesus as having authority to forgive sins (see e.g. Mark 2:5, 10//Matt 9:2, 6//Luke 5:20, 24), an authority Jesus claims as "the Son of Man". That Jesus died on a cross by crucifixion is an historical datum. That his death was an act to bring salvation to all of humanity, and a means of the forgiveness of sins, is a theological belief that cannot be established by historical examination. Nonetheless, this interpretation of the death of Jesus is a part of the claimed historical significance of the "remembered Jesus" portrayed in the gospels and the New Testament generally. We shall have to return to this aspect below.

The Son of Man.

It is an interesting phenomenon that the reference to Jesus as "the Son of Man" appears in the majority of instances on the lips of Jesus in the gospels. Elsewhere, it appears twice in reference to Jesus, once in Revelation 1:13 where John the writer recounts a vision of "the Son of Man", the glorious exalted Jesus, and again in Revelation 14:14 where the Son of Man is seated as judge on a throne ready to reap "the harvest". In both cases, this is intended to evoke the Danielic "Son of Man" (see Daniel 7:13).[124] In Acts 7: 56, as he faces an angry crowd, Stephen declares that he sees "the Son of Man standing at the right hand of God." This appears to be the only occasion when an early Christian used that descriptor of Jesus.[125] There is also an occasion in John's Gospel when others use the phrase, "Son of Man". In John 12:32–34, after Jesus has spoken of drawing all people to himself when he is "lifted up", the crowd responds by saying that they know from the law that the Messiah remains forever. So they ask: "How can you say that the Son of Man must be lifted up? Who is this Son of Man?" Thus they show that they associate the Messiah with "the Son of Man". Interestingly, Jesus has begun this discourse by referring to the "hour" when the Son of Man is to be glorified, and so the crowd must be picking up on this self-reference.[126]

In the gospels, Jesus appears to use the phrase, "the Son of Man" as a reference to himself. This is debated as it is argued that on some occasions Jesus may be referring to a "Son of Man" (probably referring to the type of "Son of Man" mentioned in Daniel 7:13) who is to come, and may be a figure other than himself. Although a case may be made for this in some instances, I think that that logic of the dialogue or discourse, the implicature if you will, often suggests that Jesus means to refer the title "Son of Man" to himself. Implicature is a speech-act term to refer to meanings that are implied by what is said, or how something is said. In the case of many "Son of Man" sayings, Jesus brings in this title in the context of saying things about himself. As an example, we might consider Mark 10:35–45, where Jesus, asked by James and John that they be given positions of honour when Jesus comes into his "glory", asks if they are able to drink the cup or undergo the baptism that he will experience (this in reference to his suffering and death). Jesus then teaches all the disciples the meaning of true discipleship, concluding with the words: "For the Son of Man came not to be served but to serve, and to give his life as a ransom for many."

Consider also Mark 2:1–12 (cf. Matt 9:1–8//Luke 5:17–26) where Jesus heals a paralysed man. When the man is lowered before Jesus by four men, Jesus first says to him, "My son, your sins are forgiven" (Mark 2:5). This leads to some scribes questioning how Jesus can say this as only God can forgive sins. Jesus, knowing this, asks them whether it is easier to forgive sins, or to tell the paralysed man to get up and walk. He then continues, "But that you may know that the Son of Man has authority on earth to forgive sins"–he said to the paralytic–"I say to you, stand up, take your mat and go to your home" (Mark 2:9, 10). Here we cannot but think that the use of the title "Son of Man" is a self-reference. I would argue that the evangelists intend every use of the title "Son of Man" in the gospels to be a self-reference by Jesus to himself.

It is widely held that the use of the phrase, "Son of Man" is authentic to the historical Jesus. This is partly because no early Christian seems to have used this as a title for Jesus. If we may accept that Jesus used this title to refer to himself, what did he mean by it? There are three possibilities put forward. One is that he meant simply to refer to a human being, or if you like, humanity in general. There is only one instance were this really applies and that is when Jesus is challenged by Pharisees over the reason why he is allowing his disciples to break the sabbath by plucking and eating grain as they walk through a grainfield (an action considered to be work by the Pharisees). Jesus concludes his answer by saying: "The sabbath was made for humankind, and not humankind for the sabbath ("humankind" translates the Greek, *ho anthrōpos,* lit. "the man", or "man", so RSV, i.e. generic "Man" in English). So the Son of Man is lord even of the sabbath" (Mark 2: 27, 28 NRSV). Some would argue that here "Son of Man" simply means "a human being"; hence we might translate: "So a human being is lord even of the sabbath". But, in that case, why use the phrase, "Son of Man"? Why not simply continue as before and say: *hōste kurios* [= lord] *estin [ho] anthrōpos tou sabbatou*: "so a man, or human being, is lord of the sabbath"?

Another explanation is that Jesus is using a third person self-reference, so that "Son of Man" means "a human like myself" or, if you will, "a man like me", perhaps even better, "someone like myself." The Aramaic term (*bar nasha*), which the Greek translates, is an idiom which can mean "someone" or may even be a kind of circumlocution for "I". An example of this usage might be when someone (Matthew's Gospel says it is a "scribe") states that he wishes to become a disciple of Jesus. Jesus replies, "Foxes have holes and birds of the air have nests; but the Son of man has nowhere to lay his head" (Matt. 8:20//Luke 9:58). Jesus clearly refers to himself: we might colloquially put it today, "this guy has nowhere to lay his head".

The question is why did Jesus choose to refer to himself in this circumlocutionary way, particularly when it gave rise to ambiguity? There seems to be no reason why Jesus, in the instance just cited, should not have simply said, "I have nowhere to lay my head." Indeed, in the very next text, when a would-be disciple asks for time to bury his father, Jesus simply says to him, "Follow me…" To answer this question, we must first consider the question of whether or not all the statements by Jesus in which he refer to "the Son of Man" are self-references, or whether in some of the statements Jesus may have another figure in view.

Scholars generally divide the Son of Man sayings in the gospels into three groups. There are those that refer to actions or circumstances of the Son of Man in the present. The sayings examined above fall into this category, that is that the Son of Man came to serve (Mark 10:45//Matt 20:28); that he is lord of the sabbath (Mark 2:28//Matt 12:8//Luke 6:5); that the Son of Man has authority to forgive sins (Mark 2:10//Matt 9:6//Luke 5:24); and that he has nowhere to lay his head (Matt 8:20//Luke 9:58). Other examples are Matt 11:19//Luke 7:34, where Jesus states that "the Son of Man came eating and drinking (in contrast to the ascetic John the Baptist), and you (his opponents) say, 'Behold, a glutton and a drunkard'"; or when Jesus speaks about his betrayal by Judas (see Mark 14:21//Matt 26:24//Luke 22:22, and cf. Mark 14:41//Matt 26:45).

In all these texts, the context shows a close relationship between some action, or situation that Jesus is involved in, where his action is closely allied to the statement about the Son of Man. Indeed, in the case of the Son of Man's authority to forgive sins, the evangelists portray Jesus's connection to the Son of Man's authority by having him challenge his critics to tell him whether it is easier to say "Your sins are forgiven" or to tell that man to "Rise and walk" (Matthew and Luke's version). He immediately instructs that man to get up and go home: in Mark and Luke, he juxtaposes the statement "that you may know that the Son of Man has authority to forgive sins" with "*I* say to you…". There is no doubt, then, that this use of the descriptor Son of Man is a self-reference.

A clear case where an evangelist understands Jesus to be making a reference to himself when using the descriptor, "Son of Man", comes in the story where Jesus asks his disciples what the general opinion is as to who he is. The group is depicted as being near Caesarea Philippi, when Matthew's Gospel has Jesus ask his disciples, "Who do people say that the Son of Man is?" (Matt 16:13). Leaving aside the fact that the disciples' replies clearly show that they understand Jesus to be referring to himself, we may note that both Mark and Luke have Jesus say, "Who do people say that *I* am?" (Mark 8:27//Luke 9:18).

A second group of texts relate to sayings about the forthcoming suffering, death and resurrection of Jesus (commonly referred to as "the passion predictions"). These sayings are repeated three times in each of the Synoptic Gospels; see Mark 8:31//Matt 16:21//Luke 9:22; Mark 9:31//Matt 17:22//Luke 9:44; Mark 10:33//Matt 20:18//Luke 18:31. In fact, on the first occasion, while Mark and Luke have Jesus refer to the Son of Man in connection with the coming suffering, death and resurrection, Matthew introduces the saying by stating: "From that time on, Jesus began to show his disciples that *he* must go to Jerusalem..." (Matt 16:21). Nevertheless, he shows that he also understands Jesus to see himself as the Son of Man, as for the second and third predictions he falls into line with Mark and Luke, as it were, and applies the sufferings to come to the Son of Man.

I think that we may fairly say, then, that with regards to the first and second groups of sayings where Jesus is using the descriptor, "Son of Man", he is referring to himself. This is the case even where there may be some ambiguity: as when Jesus states that anyone who says something against the Son of Man will be forgiven, but not when against the Holy Spirit (Matt 12:32//Luke 12:10), or when he speaks about "the sign of Jonah" (Matt 12:40), which in Matthew's Gospel might be taken as a kind of passion prediction, being a reference to his death and burial. Luke refers to Jonah as a sign of the judgment of the Son of Man (or perhaps God's judgment) on "this generation", i.e. Jesus's contemporaries for not repenting on hearing his proclamation, unlike the people of Nineveh who did repent on hearing Jonah's preaching (Luke 11:29, 30, 32). A final instance I will provide from the Synoptic Gospels is found only in Luke 19:10.[127] This comes at the end of Jesus's encounter with Zacchaeus, when Zacchaeus responds to Jesus's coming to his house, by vowing to pay back four times any amount he has defrauded anyone of, and to give half his possessions to the poor. Jesus reassures Zacchaeus, and counters the criticism of the onlookers (dismayed that Jesus has gone to the house of "a sinner"), stating that: "Today salvation has come to his house, because [Zacchaeus] too is a son of Abraham. For the Son of Man came to seek out and to save the lost." (Luke 19: 9,10).

My argument, then, is that the way in which the descriptor Son of Man is associated with things that Jesus does or what he says about the Son of Man that apply to himself, e.g. predictions about forthcoming suffering, or for that matter the way in which the Son of Man is criticised as being a glutton and a drunkard, means that the Son of Man is closely tied up with the person of Jesus. The implicit understanding that this carries is that Jesus is to be identified as the Son of Man. I would argue that this is corroborated by the way that the descriptor is used in some places in John's Gospel. As is well known, this Gospel's preferred way of speaking about Jesus is to refer to him as "the Son" (a description often placed in connection with "the Father", i.e. God). But every so often, the evangelist refers to "the Son of Man." One of these instances is in John 5:27 where he states that God ("the Father") has "given him ("the Son") authority to execute judgement, because he is the Son of Man." Here he may well have in mind such a tradition as that of Jesus's authority to forgive sin (as in the Synoptic story of the healing of the paralytic, see e.g. Mark 2:5, 10). Indeed as "the Son" has "life in himself" (John 5:26), we might see this as a reference to Jesus's healing powers: the discourse after all takes place in the context of the healing of a paralytic to whom Jesus issues the command, "Stand up, take your mat and walk" (John 5:8//Mark 2:9b, 11).[128] The references to the Son of Man being "lifted up" (a pun which associates the notion of exaltation with the "lifting up" in crucifixion) in such texts as John 3:14 and 8:28 may well be correlated with Synoptic texts referring to the death of Jesus. Thus these Son of Man statements in John's Gospel confirm that the phrase, "Son of Man", is used in self-reference.

There is, however, a third group of texts where the use of the descriptor is more ambiguous. These are texts which refer to the future coming of the Son of Man, and in these the association with Jesus may be less certain. With these texts also may be grouped those that speak of the role of the Son of Man as judge.[129] For instance, in Jesus's apocalyptic teaching in the Synoptic Gospels, Jesus refers to the coming of the Son of man, drawing upon the imagery found in Daniel 7:13, 14 (see Mark 13:26//Matt 24:30//Luke 21:27). But even here, when Jesus is speaking of the future coming, or judgment of the Son of Man, many of the statements are in a context where he is also speaking of his own person. Take, for instance, Mark 8:38//Luke 9:26 where Jesus speaks of the Son of Man being "ashamed" of anyone who has been ashamed of Jesus and his words "in this adulterous and sinful generation" (Mark). This follows immediately upon Jesus's call for disciples to follow him in the way of self-denial and cross-bearing, ready to lose one's life for Jesus's sake.[130] There is, then, a close relationship between Jesus, and response to Jesus, and acceptance or rejection by the Son of Man.

In other references to the Son of Man, however, the evangelists show that they identify Jesus as the Son of Man. For example, in Matt 19:28, in response to a statement by Peter that they have left everything to follow Jesus, Jesus replies, "Truly I tell you, at the renewal of all things, when the Son of Man is seated on the throne of his glory, you who have followed *me* will also sit on twelve thrones, judging the twelve tribes of Israel." Indeed, in Luke's Gospel, the future role of the twelve as judges of Israel is a prerogative given to them by Jesus. "You are those who have stood by me in my trials; and *I* confer on you, just as my Father has conferred on *me*, a *kingdom*, so that you may eat and drink at *my* table in *my* kingdom, and you will sit on twelve thrones judging the twelve tribes of Israel" (Luke 22:28–30). We might also note that in Matthew, the statement about sitting on twelve thrones, is immediately followed by a statement that anyone who has given up material possessions and familial relationships *"for my [Jesus's] name sake"*, will be rewarded handsomely.

A very interesting instance of the association with Jesus of the coming of the Son of Man "seated at the right hand of power and coming on the clouds of heaven" (an echo of the Danielic Son of Man passage), is Mark 14:62, which is Jesus's reply directly after he has been asked by the high priest, "Are you the Messiah, the Son of the Blessed One?" (14:61b). Jesus replies: "*I am;* and 'you will see the Son of Man seated at the right hand of the Power' and 'coming with the clouds of heaven.'" [131] In Matthew's and Luke's gospels Jesus's reply to the high priest is more ambiguous, in Matthew Jesus says "you have said it" (which might be taken either as "that's what you say" or "you've nailed it") and in Luke he throws the question back at his interlocutors by stating that even if he did affirm he was the Messiah ("if I did tell you" must surely mean a positive affirmation, although perhaps they would not believe Jesus if he denied it), they would not believe him, and would not answer if he asked them what they thought. Even here, the reference to the Son of Man, however, comes in such a way that identity of Jesus with the Son of Man is strongly implied, if not certain.

All of the Son of Man sayings seen in their broader context associate the Son of Man with Jesus.[132] Even texts such as Luke 17: 22, 26, 30; 18: 8 or Luke 21:27, where arguably there is no obvious connection with Jesus, are found in a gospel where it is clear that Jesus is to be identified with the Son of Man. For instance, in the midst of the series of references to the future coming of Son of Man in Luke 17: 22–30, comes the statement that the Son of Man must "first...endure much suffering and be rejected by *this generation*" (Luke 22:25): to whom does that refer if not Jesus? Again, between Luke 18: 8 and Luke 21:27 comes a reference to the fact that "the Son of Man came to seek out and save the lost" (Luke 19:10), of whom Zacchaeus is a representative.

It is clear, then, that the Synoptic Gospel writers consider that Jesus is to be understood using the descriptor Son of Man with reference to himself. Even John's Gospel understands Jesus to have used this descriptor of himself. Furthermore, the gospels show that the writers associated the term "Son of Man" with the Messiah. For instance, in Matt 16:13, the answer Peter gives to the question as to who the Son of Man is, is that he is the Messiah. In John's Gospel, after Jesus has healed a blind man, he asks him "Do you believe in the Son of Man?". The issue at stake earlier in the story is that of confessing that Jesus is the Messiah (9:22). Again, John has Jesus speaking about the hour having come for the Son of Man to be glorified (the Gospel's particular understanding of how Jesus's death is to be seen). In the discourse that follows, he speaks about being "lifted up". This prompts the crowd to say that they have heard "from the law that the Messiah remains forever." So how can Jesus say that the Son of Man must be lifted up? (John 12:23, 32–34). Supremely, the association is made in Mark 14:61,62, when Jesus answers the high priest's question, "Are you the Messiah (or Christ)?" by affirming that he is and then speaking immediately about the coming of the Son of Man.

It is a general consensus amongst scholars that Jesus used the descriptor, Son of Man, to refer to himself. Gerd Theissen considers it "fairly certain that Jesus used the expression *Son of Man*."[133] Indeed, Adela Yarbro Collins claims that as Jesus was seen as "a prophet of Jewish restoration eschatology or an apocalyptic prophet" it is most likely that the "apocalyptic Son of Man sayings are the oldest, that is sayings that refer to the Son of Man coming on the clouds or being revealed. The other sayings derived from these."[134] To be fair, Collins means by this, that if Jesus spoke of the apocalyptic Son of Man in reference to the figure of Daniel 7:13, then he meant someone other than himself.[135] Associating Jesus with this Son of Man was an interpretive move made subsequently by the first Christians. In fact, Mark's Gospel links the messiah with the Son of Man, and this is an association that informed hearers of the Gospel would have understood.[136]

Barnabas Lindars considers that "if Jesus used 'Son of Man' as a messianic title, it is astonishing to find that with one exception (Acts 7:56) it is never used as such in the NT other than in sayings of Jesus (or references to them)."[137] This might also be used against an argument, such as put forward by Collins, that the descriptor "Son of Man" was a creation of the early church. For if they did not favour the idea of "Son of Man" as a way of describing the Messiah, why did they place this descriptor on the lips of Jesus? Of course, Collins's position could be put up as an argument against Lindars's statement, for all the Son of Man statements created by the early church (and put on Jesus's lips) are evidence that the descriptor it is used in the New Testament as a messianic title: a title made messianic by its use in the gospels by the evangelists (or the tradition they drew upon).

So the various scholarly opinions on the use of the descriptor Son of Man in the gospels leave open two questions: if Jesus did use the descriptor "Son of Man" of himself on occasion, why did he use this circumlocution rather than speaking more directly of himself? And why did the early Christians choose to apply the concept of a heavenly Son of Man, coming in judgment at the end times, to Jesus? My argument is that Jesus did use the descriptor of himself. This is confirmed by the fact that the gospel writers, apart from at John 12:34, and Luke in his second book (Acts 7:56), always place this descriptor on the lips of Jesus. A number of the sayings can be quite easily accepted as a self-reference. If, as Collins maintains, the apocalyptic Son of Man sayings are earliest, this suggests that Jesus made a link between himself and this apocalyptic Son of Man. Nevertheless, even if some of the references are seen as an appropriation by the gospel writers (or early Christian tradition) in order to convey their understanding of Jesus's exalted, or special status as God's agent, the question remains whether this is not an appropriate interpretation of the historical significance and meaning of the historical figure. In other words, have the early Christians provided an accurate representation of the historical figure of Jesus as he truly should be understood?

If Jesus did use the descriptor, Son of Man, of himself, what did he mean by it? And did he intend to associate himself thereby with the concept of the Messiah? It would seem that Jesus was reluctant to apply the title "Messiah" to himself. However, along with others, I would maintain that Jesus's use of Son of Man was a deliberate use in order to maintain a degree of ambiguity about who he was. He wanted to avoid misunderstandings of his messiahship, such as were around in his day, but he wished to convey a view of himself that he was, indeed, a special agent of God, and, indeed, a transcendent figure with an exalted God-given status and mission. As Matthew Black states: "Although the saying in Aramaic is ambiguous, there is no doubt that the Evangelists were right in interpreting it as Messianic: Jesus intended the veiled allusion to His own identity as Son of Man."[138] Theissen considers that Jesus used the descriptor "Son of Man" to express the fact that only God could assign Jesus the role of the future Son of Man. "Jesus cannot give himself this status. He can only be certain that as the Son of Man active in the present [that is in his earthly ministry] he is carrying out God's commission on earth...Jesus' uncertainty expressed his trust in God who would assign him, a human being, an eschatological role that would make him *the* Son of Man."[139]

I would concur with Black that Jesus did use the descriptor Son of Man as a "veiled allusion", and that the early Christians were correct to see this as a confirmation that he was the Christ, as established by the fact that God raised him from the dead. While Jesus never explicitly claimed the title "Messiah", nor referred to himself as the messiah, his actions and his bold statements e.g. in forgiving sins, in associating himself with the coming Son of Man, convinced the disciples that God had made "Lord and Messiah, this Jesus whom [the Jewish authorities had caused to be] crucified" (Acts 2:36b). Furthermore, if the Danielic figure of the heavenly Son of Man had given rise to interpretations that linked this Son of Man with the Messiah, so that such a conception was "in the air" so to speak, Jesus may have picked up on that linkage.[140] Whatever the case, there is no doubt that the early Christians may well have introduced some of the instances of the use of the descriptor, "Son of Man", into the traditions about Jesus, but only because—as the evidence suggests—Jesus himself had used that descriptor of himself.[141]

The Twelve.

There is no doubt that Jesus had disciples. It is because of the continuing existence of these disciples after the crucifixion, and their witness to the resurrection, that we have the traditions that make up our New

Testament gospels. These gospels speak of an inner core of disciples chosen by Jesus and known as "the Twelve".

Athough some scholars have maintained that "the Twelve" was a creation of the early church, most accept that Jesus did choose twelve disciples to be a special group amongst the wider body of disciples. The Synoptic Gospels and the book of Acts each give a list of these disciples by name (see Matt 10:1–4//Mark 3:13–19a//Luke 6:12–16; Acts 1:13b). There is agreement amongst all the gospels on the names except in one instance. Jude [the brother/son?] of James is found only in Mark and Matthew, while Thaddeus is listed in Luke and Acts.[142] This is possibly the same individual, listed with his Greek name (Thaddeus) in Luke and Acts, and his Hebrew name (Jude) in Mark and Matthew.[143] After the resurrection, Judas Iscariot who had betrayed Jesus, was replaced by Matthias (Acts 1:15–26).

The reasons why we may accept that Jesus chose a group of disciples who were known as "the Twelve" are as follows. Both the Gospel of John and Paul refer to "the Twelve" in such a way as to suggest that this designation would be known to their readers, and they would know who was meant (see John 6:67, 70–71; 1 Cor. 15:5). John's Gospel is particularly interesting in this regard in that the evangelist seems to show little interest in referring to the group of disciples Jesus chose. Unlike the Synoptic Gospels, he does not provide either a story of Jesus choosing twelve disciples, or a list of their names.[144] However, he does identify two disciples as belonging to the twelve, Judas Iscariot (John 6:71) and Thomas (John 20:24). These two are found in the Synoptic lists of "the Twelve", as well as others mentioned by the evangelist, such as Andrew, Philip, and the two "sons of Zebedee" (see John 21:2).[145] But there are others who are mentioned who are not on the list, such as Nathanael (John 1:45–51; 21:2), and the mysterious disciple known only as "the beloved disciple".[146] Are they to be counted as part of "the Twelve"? Mostly, the evangelist refers to "Jesus and the disciples", but does not specify exactly who these disciples are. In narrative terms, we might assume that the reference is to those who are named in the first chapter, but then others emerge as disciples as well, such as "the beloved disciple", and "the sons of Zebedee". The Gospel writer is more interested in disciples being those who believe in Jesus, and follow him, or accept his claims about himself (see his exchange with "the Twelve" in John 6:66–71, where many disciples are deserting him on account of his teaching being too hard to accept).[147] So, as far as this Gospel is concerned, others may be included in the discipleship band, such as the anonymous blind man in John 9; Joseph of Arimathea, and, possibly, Nicodemus (I think, probably, but both these two fall under some censure by the evangelist for being "secret" disciples, see John 20:38–42; cf. John 12:42, 43).

Other reasons, apart from the mention of "the Twelve" in John's Gospel and 1 Corinthians 15 (so this datum is multiply attested), are that the Twelve do not feature as a group otherwise in the New Testament era post-resurrection. This would hardly be the case if this group was a post-resurrection development. Furthermore, the argument is made that the presence of the name, Judas Iscariot, the betrayer, in the lists is an indication that this group existed prior to the death of Jesus. On balance it is difficult to provide an adequate reason for why the early Christians would invent a tradition about "the Twelve" over against the likelihood that the twelve disciples were chosen by Jesus to fulfil a particular role.[148]

Given that Jesus chose twelve disciples, what was his purpose in doing so? First of all, Jesus chose twelve as a symbol of the coming kingdom of God and the hoped for restoration of the twelve tribes of Israel. E. P. Sanders states that by this choice of "the Twelve", "Jesus intended to show that he had in view the full restoration of the people of Israel."[149] In Matthew 19:28, Jesus tells the twelve disciples that they will sit on twelve thrones judging the twelve tribes of Israel. In Luke 22:29, 30, Jesus says "I confer on you, just as my Father has conferred on me, a kingdom, so that you may eat and drink at my table in my kingdom, and you will sit on thrones judging the twelve tribes of Israel" (in Matthew Jesus refers to himself as the Son of Man). The book of Revelation picks up the idea that the twelve disciples (or apostles) feature as important figures in the coming kingdom when in its vision of the "new Jerusalem", the writer says that, "the wall of the city has twelve foundations, and on them are the twelve names of the twelve apostles of the Lamb" (Rev. 21:14).

The story of Jesus's choice of the twelve disciples indicates some of the further roles that they were to fulfil. Mark 13:14 says that they were "to be with him", being taught by him and learning from him: in this respect they were first and foremost disciples (learners under a teacher, or rabbi) during Jesus's ministry. But they were also called "apostles": that is they were sent out by Jesus to share in his work of proclaiming the kingdom. They were also given authority to cast out evil spirits: an aspect of Jesus's work that Mark particularly emphasises, as it shows the kingdom of God coming to overcome and break the power of Satan (see Mark 3:19b–27).[150]

Matthew's account of the sending out of the apostles has Jesus instructing them to restrict their mission to the "house of Israel" only. This seems to be in line with his own understanding of his mission which was to "the lost sheep of the house of Israel" (see Matt. 15:21–28, cf. Mark 7:24–30). In both Matthew's and Mark's Gospels there is a cutting remark made to a Canaanite/Syrophoenician woman to the effect that the children's bread should not be fed to the dogs (Matt. 15:26//Mark 7:27). Nonetheless, Jesus responded to this woman's request to heal her daughter. Jesus interacted with non-Jewish persons on several other occasions. While the focus of his attention was upon Israel, after the resurrection Jesus is shown to tell his disciples to widen their outreach to the wider, non-Jewish world (see Matt. 28:16–20; Acts 1:8 cf. Luke 24:47).

Eckhard Schnabel notes two important functions of the twelve apostles that, taken together, underline the fact that they provide a link between the Jesus who lived and worked among them prior to his crucifixion, and the risen Jesus whom they proclaimed as Lord and Messiah. These two functions are closely related: they are that (1) the twelve apostles were authoritative eyewitnesses to the historical Jesus's life, and (2) that they were authoritative transmitters of the Jesus tradition.[151]

On the first function, Schnabel notes that their role as witnesses to the resurrection was particularly important, and a central aspect for Luke. He states that "it is central both in the description of the criteria of apostleship when the need arose to replace Judas Iscariot (Acts 1:21–22) and in Peter's preaching and teaching (Acts 2:32; 3:15; 4:2, 10, 33; 5:32; 10:41)."[152] Their role as witnesses generally is not only confirmed in their post-resurrection commissioning by Jesus (Luke 24:47; Acts 1:8, and implicitly in Matt. 28:19, 20), but it is also foreshadowed, as it were, by the author of John's Gospel in Jesus's "high priestly prayer" when Jesus prays, "I ask [that the disciples be sanctified in truth] not only on behalf of these, but also on behalf of those who will believe in me through their word..." (John 17:20). Note also that Jesus has earlier said that the Advocate, the Spirit of truth will testify on Jesus's behalf, and that the disciples also are to testify because they have been with him from the beginning (John 15:26, 27).

As far as the second function is concerned, I am persuaded by Birger Gerhardsson's argument that the Twelve formed a kind of group that concentrated on handing on the traditions about Jesus.[153] They were the "eyewitnesses and servants of the word" (Luke 1:2) that Luke refers to in the prologue to his gospel. When the problem of caring for the widows of the Hellenists arose (Acts 6:1–6), and the Twelve said that they should not "neglect the word of God in order to wait on tables" (6:2), so that seven deacons were chosen for the task, the "serving the word" that the Twelve were engaged in was teaching and preaching about Jesus, including passing on what they had heard from him. In addition, they were continuing to form and develop their understanding of who Jesus was as they studied their scriptures.[154] If what Luke says in Acts 6:7 about "a great many priests" joining the nascent Jesus movement may be taken as historically accurate, I expect that many of these would have been also engaged with the Twelve (and others) in scriptural studies.

At any rate, there were those, in addition to the Twelve, who remembered and passed on teaching of Jesus, and stories about what he did. Some of these perhaps also shaped what we might call "traditions about Jesus" and linked these to their scriptures. We should not forget that the evangelists themselves have played a major role in shaping the Jesus traditions in written form that we know as our gospels. They did not simply receive traditions from others, but arranged them and plotted their narratives to bring out the particular understanding of Jesus, and of being disciples of Jesus, that they wished to convey. The historical Jesus that we read about, and scholars research today, is refracted through the lenses provided by the reminiscences, the memories, the shaped traditions of the first Christians. The remembered and "handed on", or testified to, Jesus is the only Jesus we have access to. This does not necessarily mean that the historical Jesus and the remembered Jesus as refracted through the gospel narratives are as far apart from each other as some scholars would have us believe. Nor does it mean that the historical significance placed upon the historical person of Jesus by the early church is a misleading or incorrect understanding of who the historical Jesus was, and understood himself to be.

CHAPTER FIVE

Conclusion: The Historical, Historic Christ as the Jesus of Faith

"The Twelve", the disciples and followers of Jesus (some of whose names we know, and others who remain anonymous), believed that Jesus, the one whom they had known before his death, was from God, was a special agent of God whom they understood as "the Messiah" (or Christ). They proclaimed him as such, and referred to him as their Lord. Others through their proclamation of him also became believers; and in some cases, such as Paul, as a result of some sort of encounter with the Risen Jesus.

The catalyst for their beliefs was the resurrection. This threw the life and death of Jesus of Nazareth, the historical person that they had known into a new light. Things that he had done and said took on a new meaning. They understood him, and the meaning of his life and death in a way that they had only begun to grasp dimly while he was still alive. As they reflected on his life and death, as they tried to make sense of their experience of him in the light of the resurrection and in examination of their scriptures, they also recalled his deeds and words and passed them on to others. Their memories were refracted through their new understanding of who he was. They were not simply interested in relating stories about Jesus, but in conveying what they understood to be the significance of his life and death, and, indeed, his very person.

Eventually these memories and interpreted reflections came to be captured in written form and handed down in the form of writings we call gospels. Our difficulty as historians and as believers coming to these gospel writings is that we really do not know how they came to be as they were. There is a gap between the death and resurrection of Jesus, and the time when the disciples first began to proclaim their beliefs in Jesus as the Christ, and the appearance of the gospels that we can only fill by creating hypotheses, making guesses (many educated guesses to be sure) and essentially speculating on how these gospels came about. However, they form the main sources from which we reconstruct the life of the historical person, Jesus, to whom they witness.

It is my guess, or hypothesis if you will, that the gospels came to us much more directly from the disciples, for example, Peter in the case of Mark's Gospel, "the beloved disciple" (whoever he was) in the case of John's Gospel, than often thought. The gospel writers, however, took the material that they received (whether directly from a disciple, or from oral traditions) and shaped them into the connected narratives that we now have. What they have provided us with, how the gospels came together, and how we assess them are also part of the difficulty and challenge of trying to fill the gap between the events recorded and the time of writing. All this is the stuff of historical reconstruction.

The Resurrection as Catalyst.

The resurrection as an "event" is a difficulty for historians and a puzzle for all who try to understand it as something that happened within history or the ordinary course of daily human life as seen in retrospect. In some ways, it is a unique event much as is the "Big Bang" or the disappearance of the dinosaurs. What we have are the "after effects": in the case of the dinosaurs, fossilized evidence of their existence, and bones here and there. We then hypothesise that they were wiped out by, or in the aftermath of, a meteor hitting the earth. There may even be geological evidence of this. But it remains a hypothesis, and it is possible that their disappearance is due a period of adverse climate change (with or without a meteoric cause).

In the case of the resurrection, the "after effects" are testimonies by people who followed Jesus stating that they discovered an empty tomb, and that many of them had some sort of encounter with Jesus which convinced them that he had been raised from the dead. Because of these experiences and their conviction that God, having raised Jesus from the dead, had made him both Lord and Messiah, and through their proclamation of Jesus as such, we have accounts of the "remembered Jesus" (to borrow a phrase coined by James Dunn). A further "after effect" is, of course, the existence and growth of a movement that derived from their experiences and accounts of what they proclaimed had happened to Jesus, and what this meant for understanding his historic significance.

Now, these testimonies to the resurrection, and the accounts of the "remembered Jesus" are open to different interpretations and historical reconstructions. For Reimarus the account of the resurrection was a deception, and the proclamation of Jesus as the Christ and "the saviour of the world" was a creation of the disciples. A "default setting" that has arisen partly out of Reimarus's work is that there is a need to distinguish between the historical person of Jesus and the church's proclamation and belief in him as the Christ.[155] Scholars and historians then settle along a spectrum of decision-making as to how much of the material can reliably been attributed to the historical person of Jesus, and how much to the creativity of the early church.

There are several ironies in this situation. One is that, by and large, historians who want to try and reconstruct Jesus are more-or-less obliged, by the nature of the sources available to them, to rely on the testimony and writings of the followers of Christ to create their reconstruction. Hence, there is a great deal of effort and industry expended upon putting the testimony and writings to the question (using it against the testifiers in a sense) and trying to find criteria to distinguish what can be trusted as historical and what is created material which is, *ipso facto*, untrustworthy. A further irony, as it seems to me, is that the more material that is deemed untrustworthy, and unusable for reconstructing the historical Jesus, the less cogent become the reasons for attributing any historical importance to him.

It is also ironic, and for Christians who believe in a God who does act within the confines of human activity and this planet's history it is a difficulty, that historical reconstruction can make no place for acts of God, such as resurrection. This raises the question of whether a case can be made for the place of belief in historical reconstruction.

History and Belief.

The historical sources, then, for our reconstruction of the life, death, and (claimed) resurrection of Jesus are the testimonies of the early Christians, the first followers of Jesus, especially those who lived with him, spent time with him and were his contemporaries. What we have, however, are their memories as remembered, as refracted through their retrospective viewpoints (the Gospel of John especially makes this clear, see John 2:27; 12:16).[156] Furthermore, these memories and testimonies have been handed down through oral tradition, and in written accounts which themselves are the result of the creative, and purposeful shaping and ordering (the plotting, to put it in terms of narrative criticism) of their implied authors, whom we conventionally call "the Evangelists". All this means that, as historical sources, they are "committed" testimony and the "remembered Jesus" they give us is a figure in whom the conveyors of his story have put their belief and trust.

What does this mean for their use as sources for history? We have seen that for historians, and scholars studying the historical Jesus, this means that they must be subject to critical analysis. The purpose of this analysis is to separate out what may be accepted as usable for historical reconstruction (always remembering that the reconstruction is the "history" not the data extracted from the sources themselves), and what is to be considered theological interpretation.[157] There is, I contend, a trap here into which much scholarship has fallen: it is to create a divide between "history" and "theology", so that what can be classified as "historical" is a true representation of the historical Jesus, while what is "theology" is at best to be left in a category called "theological" (not necessarily "untrue" but not somehow a representation of the historical Jesus); at worst, what is "theological" is seen as "untrue", certainly not historically reliable.

We must distinguish here between what might be termed "purely theological" (that is beyond the purview and interests of "history") and what may be accepted as a "form of history", or what I would call "theologised history". To say that the purpose of the death of Jesus was salvific: that, for instance, "Jesus died for the sins of the world", or even, "Jesus died for my sins", is a purely theological statement in that it cannot be established as a piece of historical datum: it is not a statement that an historian can make, only one that can be made by a believer.[158]

However, to say that "Jesus was raised from the dead" is potentially a historical claim. This is because the evidence, the "after effects" of the "resurrection event", may mean that to say that the resurrection happened within history, within the confines of that part of the space-time continuum that is this planet earth, is to make the best sense of the evidence. On the other hand, the claims that Christians say are consequent upon this "event", that Jesus is the Son of God, the Messiah, and so forth, move into the realm of "pure theology".

Nonetheless, there is a proviso to be raised here. It has to do with the interpretive nature of historical discourse. That is to say, to say that in the life, death, and resurrection of Jesus the historical figure God was at work: or to put it in the starkest terms of orthodox Christian belief, that the historical figure of Jesus was God incarnate, is to provide a historical interpretation. Because God is brought into the historical interpretation, it is an interpretation that stands outside of the conventionally accepted canons of historical discourse (secular history, if you will). Thus the story of Jesus presented by the Gospel writers is "theologised history" insofar as it provides historical data. It is an interpretation of the historical Jesus based on theological understandings and the premise that, in Jesus, God has entered the affairs of this world. My argument is that this must be allowed to stand as a "form of history". It may be a true representation of Reality; it may be a historical account that best captures the nature and person of the historical figure who lived in a corner of this world at a given point in time.[159]

Because of the nature of historical discourse as it has developed in the west since the Enlightenment, as a "form of history" the interpretation of Jesus that arises from this can only be one interpretation alongside others. Historians, depending upon their own belief systems and viewpoints, will assess the data differently, will make different judgments upon the reliability or otherwise of that data. Also, because "theologised history", the form of history that I am advocating, is a committed form of history, that is, it depends upon belief and faith commitments as well as historical analysis, its historical judgments and interpretation cannot be what may be universally accepted by historians everywhere.[160] I do not claim that it should. I wish to claim that as a "form of history" it should be given space to stand alongside other forms of history on equal ground. It will not be universally accepted as the historical explanation of the historical Jesus, but it ought to be allowed to stand as one among others.

The historical Jesus as the historical, historic Christ: a reprise.

The historical Jesus came onto the scene in Palestine preaching the kingdom of God and presenting as a prophet in the mould of the ancient prophets, calling the people (as John the Baptist had done) to a renewal of life that truly reflected the values and lifestyle affirmed by their covenant God. He demonstrated his authority as an agent of God by "wonderful deeds", and especially the power of the kingdom over forces of evil through performing exorcisms. He had a style of teaching that captured imaginations, often conveyed through pithy tales drawing on everyday life (parables), or in brief aphorisms, proverbs, and maxims. He also reframed aspects of the law to draw out their inner essence and intention. How much he engaged in extended teaching and discourses is uncertain (this may be a function of the evangelists', especially Matthew's organising of the material).[161] We do not know the content (apart from a few snippets) of the "private teaching" that Jesus is reported to have given to his disciples.

Along the way, Jesus spoke of himself as "the Son of Man", a manner of speaking of himself that was suggestive, but ambiguous. Some of his statements made claims that indicated that he believed he had a special relationship with God his Father, and a special mission given to him by God. He certainly was prepared to have people see him as a prophet; and though he never encouraged anyone to identify him as the Messiah (and certainly resisted any attempts to manipulate his agenda), he did not outright deny this role when his disciples suggested that this was what he was. Prior to his death, he instituted a special act of commemoration (it may or may not have been during a Passover meal), which suggested that he saw his death as somehow redemptive and salvific for those who were attached to him. During his peripatetic ministry he certainly indicated that he believed that the kingdom of God was open to all sorts, including those considered religiously impure, "sinners", and others who were marginalised, or despised in Jewish society at the time.

He fell foul of the religious authorities, who considered some of his teaching and actions as blasphemous. He also had occasional altercations and debates with other groups in society such as the Pharisees, or the Sadducees. In the end, and particularly after two dramatic prophetic acts which are portrayed as a triumphal entry into Jerusalem, and an action in the Temple (a "cleansing", prophetic protest against temple practices, or prophetic of the temple's destruction, the motivation is disputed by historians), the Jewish authorities moved against him. Convicted on a charge of blasphemy, and when brought before Pilate as the Roman authority with power to put Jesus to death, a charge of treasonous claims to be the "the king of the Jews", Jesus was crucified.

Shortly thereafter, according to the testimony and claims of his followers, his tomb was discovered to be empty, and a number of his disciples (at one time, according to a tradition handed on by Paul, as many as five hundred) had encounters with Jesus that convinced them that he had been raised from the dead: "God had raised him up" was how they understood this to have come about. In the light of these experiences, their understanding of who Jesus was, and his historic significance, shifted, or expanded, dramatically. They now were certain that Jesus was the Messiah, who would come again to finally establish God's kingdom. They also rapidly began to affirm him as their Lord, and as one who was God. The deeds he had done during his ministry became "proofs", "signs" the evangelist who wrote John's Gospel called them, of his status both as Messiah and Lord.

They recalled his actions and words at their last meal with him (what we now know as "the Lord's Supper", Holy Communion or the Eucharist) and they came to understand that Jesus's death was in some way, variously described in their reflections captured in the New Testament, as a death on their behalf, bringing them forgiveness of sin, salvation and new life. "…the Son of God who loved me and gave himself for me" (Gal 2:20) was how Paul put it, or in another place, "But God proves his love for us in that while we were still sinners Christ died for us" (Romans 5:8). The evangelist Mark wrote, "For the Son of Man came not to be served but to serve, *and to give his life a ransom for many.*" (Mark 10:45).[162] The writer to the Hebrews, reflecting on the Jewish sacrificial system, and the role of the high priest, saw Jesus as "merciful and faithful high priest in the service of God, to make atonement for the sins of the people" (Heb. 2:17b), making it clear later in the epistle that this was through his death (Heb. 9:11–14, 26; 10:10).

The "remembered Jesus" as captured in the gospels, and the risen Christ as witnessed to in the preaching of the early Christians (and writings of the New Testament) are one and the same historical person. Jesus as remembered and preached may not be exactly the same as the Jesus who lived in first-century Palestine. That person is part of the past: he can only be reconstructed by historians. Remembered Jesus or reconstructed Jesus are the only historical Jesuses we can have. What the early Christians have given us is the historical Jesus in his historic significance, according to how they remembered and have experienced him, and in the light of their faith and trust in that significance: a significance arrived at as they saw the remembered historical person in the light of an amazing "event", the resurrection.

APPENDIX

Once the view had taken hold that the Gospels, as repositories of the early Christian beliefs about Jesus meant that they had to be subject to critical analysis to enable the historian to separate out, as it were, the authentic material deriving from the historical Jesus from the overlay of Christological beliefs, there was felt a necessity to define criteria by which this process of separation could take place.

Although a number of these criteria developed after the Second World War, and are said to derive from the work of the form critics, I maintain that the roots of the problem lie further back in the "bifurcation" of the understanding of the pre-Easter Jesus as opposed to the post-Easter Jesus proclaimed by the early Christians (this is often called the issue of "the Jesus of history" versus "the Christ of faith").[163] Although Jens Schröter claims form criticism as the "methodological foundation" for the development of the criteria, he recognises the ideological roots in the "bifurcation" of the search for the Jesus of history from the "theological narratives" deriving from the early Christian's faith. He captures this neatly in a paragraph that is worth quoting in full. He writes:

> The perspective on the Gospels as theological narratives has also resulted in the opposition of kerygma [viz. early Christian preaching/proclamation of Jesus as the Christ] and history. It has been argued that the faith of earliest Christianity has imposed its character on the historical data and must therefore be distinguished from Jesus' words and deeds themselves. As a consequence, a bifurcation arose between those who–*from Reimarus to Crossan, Funk, and the Jesus Seminar*–emphasize the need to recover the "real" events behind the misinterpretations and corruptions by the early Christians on the one hand and those who–*from Kähler to Bultmann and Johnson*–stress the importance of the Christian kerygma as the sole basis for an access to the meaning of Jesus. This is also the *context* for the establishment of the "criteria" in historical Jesus research. It emerged as a critical tool to secure a minimum of "authentic" Jesus tradition from its interpretation in earliest Christianity and at the same time from ancient Judaism as the cultural and religious context of Jesus.[164]

The last sentence of the above quotation mentions the first of the criteria, what has been called the criterion of "double dissimilarity". This criterion maintains that we may accept a tradition about Jesus (whether it is something he said or something he did) as "authentic", that is, historically reliable, if it neither derives from the Judaism of the day (that is Second Temple Judaism in and around the first century), nor from the early Church (that is, something that might actually be a creation of the early church that has "read back onto", or placed upon the historical Jesus). Long ago, it was pointed out that we simply did not know enough about either Second Temple Judaism, or the early church, to be certain about what was dissimilar from either of these. Furthermore, the Jesus that emerged from the use of this criterion was not a characteristic Jesus but rather an idiosyncratic Jesus, a Jesus who neither fitted into his first century context, nor had any influence upon the movement that stemmed from him.[165]

A second, and related, criterion is that called "embarrassment", that is, material that the early Christians would find "embarrassing" or cause them discomfort because it did not fit with their view of Jesus; or would create difficulties in their preaching of Jesus as the Christ and Son of God. John P. Meier appears to favour this criterion, and refers to it quite frequently in his presentation of Jesus.[166]

The parade example of an incident seen as embarrassing to the early Christians is the baptism of Jesus by John the Baptist. Why would the early Christians preserve a tradition about Jesus that appeared to subordinate a "sinless" Jesus, who is Son of God, to John the Baptist, and to a baptism representing repentance from sin? Furthermore, the gospels, if we analyse the account from Mark's Gospel through Matthew and Luke to John, appear to attempt to side-step the problem by explaining it (away?) in Matthew, to downplaying it or writing it out of the narrative in Luke and John.[167]

As I see it there are a number of difficulties with this, leaving aside the question of what would "embarrass" an early Christian community that appears, in the opinion of many scholars, quite happy to create stories about Jesus, and recount stories that put the disciples (leaders of the early Christian community) in a poor light.[168] For a start, the argument of a developing reticence to attribute the baptism of Jesus to John the Baptist assumes the priority of Mark's Gospel to the others. If this proved not to be the case, a major plank in the argument would disappear.

Even if we do accept the priority of Mark, and it must be said that it is a majority opinion amongst scholars, and one I accept as making good sense of the "Synoptic Problem," alternative motivations for the evangelists' treatment might be provided. We cannot assume that the rhetorical ploys of the evangelists necessarily arise out of "embarrassment". Matthew, for instance, may see the exchange between Jesus and John the Baptist as actually enhancing Jesus's status in the mind of the reader, and also as a way of showing that Jesus fits into the theme of "[fulfilling] all righteousness". Luke, in relating the story of John's preaching that challenged his hearers' wrongdoing, adds that one function of it was to rebuke King Herod for his marriage to Herodias. So Luke immediately mentions the consequence of John's opposition to Herod's marriage which was John's imprisonment (hence it is a logical place to mention this, or if you wish it is a digression). He then goes on to speak of Jesus's baptism. Placed where it is, a logical conclusion is that John would have been the one to have baptised him. The statement is that Jesus is also baptised along with "all the people" (viz. those who had been coming to John for baptism). Implicature suggests that this belongs with the previous account, particularly when some of the features (such as the descent of the Spirit and the voice from heaven) evoke the Markan account. Even if it appears that Luke is avoiding stating explicitly that John the Baptist baptised Jesus, it remains the case that he makes it clear that Jesus was baptised. The historian would need to explain why, and what the nature of this baptism may have been.

As for John's Gospel, the debate is an open one regarding whether or not the evangelist knew the Synoptic traditions (possibly Mark's tradition), or at least a pre-Synoptic tradition. He may simply be taking knowledge of Jesus's baptism by John for granted, preferring to highlight John's role as a witness to Jesus (hence, for instance, John 1:24–27, where he picks up the tradition of John's statement about being unworthy to untie the thong of the sandal of the one coming after him, cf. Mark 1:7//Matt. 3:11//Luke 3:16). The writer of John's Gospel certainly seems to presuppose prior knowledge of John the Baptist's activities, his preaching and his fate: see his almost "throw-away" comment in John 3:24, "John, of course, had not yet been thrown into prison" (NRSV).[169] Nothing has been said prior to this comment about John's imprisonment, and nothing is related later. Whether the evangelist is relying on general knowledge about John the Baptist, or presupposing knowledge of the Synoptic traditions about John is difficult to say. The evangelist evokes, or hints at, interesting details that can be corroborated, and expanded upon, by reference to the Synoptic accounts, such as the aforementioned statement about the untying of sandals, as well as a reference to the descent of the Spirit upon the one John witnesses to (identified now as Jesus, "the Lamb of God"), and the fact that Jesus will baptise with the Holy Spirit.

A further consideration is the fact that the early church practiced baptism. However, as far as I am aware, no scholar regards this as a reason to cast doubt on the baptism of Jesus in that it is not "dissimilar" from early Christian practice. One might surely argue that having an account of Jesus's baptism would bolster the early Christian practice and hence serve to legitimate post-Easter Christian tradition.

All-in-all, I would argue, an argument such as the one that is often mounted for the "embarrassment" provided by the tradition of John the Baptist's baptising of Jesus, may be explained in other ways, such as by analysing the rhetorical effects that the evangelists are striving for in their respective accounts. Other criteria such as traces of Aramaic in the gospels (and parts of the gospel accounts that may purportedly be recast into Aramaic) and narrative that portray a Palestinian environment, may be dismissed as possibly due to the fact that these traditions arose initially in an Aramaic-speaking church located in Palestine. The problem is, of course, that all our sources arose out of the post-Easter preaching, reflection and faith of the earliest Christians. Once the position is taken that they are, therefore, suspect as providing reliable information about the historical Jesus, then the ground very quickly liquefies under the historian's feet. This is not to say that they should not be subject to critical analysis, but it does show, as scholarship is increasingly understanding and showing (see the contributions to *Jesus, Criteria, and the Demise of Authenticity*), that the criteria for authenticating what is historical in the search for the historical Jesus are not fit for purpose.

Two of the criteria, if used with proper understanding and care, however, are simply tools that all historians of whatever stripe use, both secular and Jesus researchers. One is "multiple attestation", which is simply the use of sources independent of one another to garner data where there is agreement, or what might be called "corroborative evidence", between, or among the sources. The other is "coherence", provided this is understood, not as providing material that "coheres" with data that has been established as "authentic" on the basis of the use of other criteria, but rather "coherence" as providing data that enables the historian to fit Jesus into his context, and to explain his affect and influence upon his followers.[170]

In this regard, there have been attempts to improve upon the criteria by providing another philosophical, or epistemological basis upon which to assess the data in the sources. One has been developed by Gerd Theissen and Dagmar Winter, and may be described as the criterion of the historically plausible Jesus. That is the reconstruction of Jesus must both place him plausibly within his first century Jewish context, while retaining a picture of a distinct individual within that context. On the other hand, traditions that derive from the (early Christian) sources (which are part of the "historical effects" of the historical Jesus), can be accepted as plausibly indicative of what Jesus said or did if they are in tension with what the early Christians believed about Jesus, or are "repeatedly found despite the variety of tendencies in different streams of early Christianity".[171] They themselves call this "the criterion of historical plausibility".[172] It seems to me that in attempting to revise the criterion of dissimilarity as traditionally held, they have tipped the balance in favour of a Jewish Jesus, who stands over against the early Christians' beliefs in him.[173] This may be problematic in that many, if not most, of the earliest Christians were themselves Jews, and the sources themselves betray much influence of the Hebrew Scriptures, not to mention Jewish concepts such as "Messiah". Are Theissen and Winter in danger of removing earliest Christianity too far from its Jewish roots? Furthermore, the way that they apply the criterion seems to highlight the idiosyncratic Jesus as regards his influence upon early Christianity.

N. T. Wright also attempts a revision of the criterion of dissimilarity by way of an addition to the criterion. He writes: "Along with the much-discussed 'criterion of dissimilarity' must go a criterion of double similarity: when something can be seen to be credible (though perhaps deeply subversive) within first-century Judaism, *and* credible as the implied starting-point (though not the exact replica) of something in later Christianity, there is a strong possibility of our being in touch with the genuine history of Jesus."[174] This seems more hopeful in terms of retaining a Jewish Jesus who also influenced his earliest Jewish followers.

Stanley Porter in his book *The Criteria for Authenticity in Historical-Jesus Research*, proposes that as Greek was the *lingua franca* in Palestine in Jesus's time, and as it is likely that Jesus himself understood and even spoke Greek on occasion in certain contexts, it might be possible to recover actual words of Jesus preserved within the Greek gospels.[175] In my opinion, his proposal still suffers from the idea that we can somehow excavate the historical Jesus from the text of the gospels, rather like digging out an artefact and scraping all the dirt and detritus off it until we have retrieved the item in its original state.[176]

Can we find another approach that dispenses with the criteria?

As the book, *Jesus, Criteria, and the Demise of Authenticity* edited by Keith and Le Donne attests, there has been much discussion in recent years about whether and in what ways the criteria for authenticity may be dispensed with. But, if we do not have the criteria to use, even if adapted as Theissen and Winter, or others have proposed, how may we achieve our reconstruction of the historical Jesus?

This, of course, begs the question of which historical Jesus we wish to reconstruct, and perhaps even whose historical Jesus we are after. However, leaving that aside for the moment, we remain with the question of methodology. In this century there has been an increasing interest in what may be called "memory studies", and in particular the role that social memory may play in forming the traditions, or if you will memories of Jesus and how these have been passed on. This is possibly a fruitful development: however, social memory theory may be applied in a number of ways, and in one mode (what has been called a "presentist" model) the needs and interests of the present adapt the "memories" of the past so much to the present, that, it seems to me, the past is more a construction out of the present than a recovery of the past. Indeed, in this mode, the memories of Jesus are, in the hands of some scholars, the creation of the early Christians out of scripture or on the basis of some sort of "type"; e.g. the deaths of Jewish prophets.[177] In some respects, this use of social memory aligns with the approach of the form critics; and as an understanding of the relation of the historical Jesus to the church's belief in him, stands in the tradition of Reimarus.

Some scholars refer to "collective memory", which is perhaps another term for social memory, though in some respects, some who use this term, seem to adhere more closely to a sense of a connection between actual memories and early Christian belief and practice.[178] I shall leave further exploration of the use of memory to one side, partly because it is such a large field of discussion and debate (some of which, I find, can be based on theorizing that is quite difficult to get to grips with), and more particularly because I do not have a good grasp of the topic. Suffice to say that I find the use of memory by J.D.G Dunn in his *Jesus Remembered* compelling. Briefly, he holds that variations in events narrated in the Synoptic Gospels, for instance, arise because of the flexibility in the oral transmission of the stories. Drawing on Kenneth Bailey's discussion of *haflat samar*, in which the mode of transmission is informal, but controlled, Dunn demonstrates how a number of Synoptic stories have the same core, and often significant shared wording, but often vary in the details: features of oral transmission.[179] But "clearly the same story is being retold".[180] His insistence that the only Jesus we can have access to is the "remembered Jesus" (captured in the written Gospels that have come down to us) is a foundational insight.[181]

My own approach is, perhaps, more impressionistic, and looks for a broad brush, general, and plausible reconstruction of the historical Jesus. It looks for what may be seen as characteristic of Jesus (and this respect has some affinities with the approaches of Dunn, Theissen and Winter, and others). I am taken with this comment by Morna Hooker.

> As with an expressionist painting, what we need to do is stand back from it, rather than poring over details, for the closer we get, the less we see of the whole. If we concentrate on the whole rather than the details, however, we shall find we know quite a lot about Jesus, even though we may not be able to reconstruct with certainty any of his sayings or actions.[182]

So, I look for broad agreements in the gospels. I attempt to see these against the backdrop of Jesus's context, and most particularly in the light of his standing in line with the prophets of the Old Testament. I think, too, that what I isolate as important for understanding the historical Jesus arises from broad agreements amongst scholars: in, for instance, Jesus's preaching and teaching the kingdom (or reign of God), in his use of parables, aphorisms and pithy sayings, in his performance of exorcisms, in his healing activities, in his association with those on the margins of Jewish society.

A bridge too far?

However, when I seek to bring in the resurrection as an item in the reconstruction of the historical Jesus, am I going too far? Am I trying to bring a faith-based approach into what should remain a (strictly secular?) historical discipline? Am I mixing up theology with history?

In a sense, the answer is "Yes" and "No". Under the conventions of modern historiography since the Enlightenment, and as I have argued in the main body of this book, following the divide created between the historical Jesus and the early Christians' faith in him, certain claims for Jesus have been labelled "theological", as it were, and others are seen as "historical". In a hermeneutical reflection on the problems of historical research for Christian faith, Gerd Theissen writes:

> All knowledge of Jesus is…more or less hypothetical. It is, in the best case, 'plausible.' With regard to historical reconstruction, one can always say, 'It could be some other way.' But faith [which he sees as "unconditional certainty"] says apodictically, 'This is the way it is.' The problem is, How can conditional historical knowledge provide the basis for an unconditional certainty?[183]

I think that there is a problem with claiming "unconditional certainty" for faith.[184] My argument is that the interpretative nature of history allows for a "theological interpretation" of historical events that is "plausible". The Christian historian may say, "This interpretation of the historical Jesus, that includes the faith claims made for Jesus by the earliest Christians in the light of the resurrection, is the most plausible interpretation in my opinion." There will, of course, be other interpretations: other "plausible" hypotheses put forward. My claim, however, is that there is no reason why a "theologised history" may not stand alongside other forms of history.

Given the short space of time within which the fundamental beliefs of the early Christians came about, it seems to me entirely plausible that (a) an event such as the resurrection precipitated the understanding of the historical Jesus that they promulgated, and (b) that their interpretation of the Jesus they remembered may be taken to be an entirely "plausible" interpretation of who he is, and that this interpretation may stand as a historical interpretation.

Coda.

I accept that in my account I have provided little argumentation for the claim that a "high Christology" (to give it its technical name) was early, and arrived at within a short space of time after Jesus's death by crucifixion. Others have made that case far more cogently than I can. It seems to me that had the belief in Jesus as the Messiah, Son of God, whom God raised from the dead, developed over a long period of time, then the earliest documents would contain far more variety than they do. The same applies to "traditions" that are being "freely invented" by a creative early Christian community. The canonical gospels would have been far more fanciful, as some of the later non-canonical gospels tend to be. The canonical gospels are remarkable also for their literary quality, and, I maintain, provide a remarkably coherent story of Jesus, especially given the "incoherence" of their theological claims. By "incoherence" I mean the difficulty that their claims about this historical Jesus creates for historical, and even what might be thought to be "rational", thought. For fundamentally they claim the activity of God within history, indeed, the involvement of God in human form in human history. This means, of course, that there is a "transcendent" and extra-terrestrial dimension to the history that derives from the acts of God: both incarnation and resurrection. This creates a difficulty for Christian historians in the field of historiography as it has evolved in recent centuries. However, it does not remove the possibility that Christian theological and Gospel explanations for the "Christ event" do not make a "plausible" explanation (in terms of an adequate and sensible account) of the evidence (which, in any case, remains puzzling for historians of any stripe).

Nor is it necessarily the case that, in terms of the evidence, or the "history of the effects" of the historical Jesus, that it is entirely without types of analogy. There are other types of "one off" events that are, or must be taken to be, historical in that they impinge upon the real historical world. I have mentioned the Big Bang, and the extinction of the dinosaurs. To take this latter case, we must accept the existence of dinosaurs because physical, fossilized remains have been turned up. Why there are no longer dinosaurs upon the earth, and part of real historical time, is a matter of (a degree of) speculation. The hypothesis most favoured is that they were the victims of the aftermath of an asteroid strike. It might be possible to mount a different hypothesis: for example, that there was no asteroid strike, but that they died out as a result of a period of adverse climate change. However, the continuing existence of the descendants of the dinosaurs, such as the birds and certain lizards (e.g. here in New Zealand the tuatara) might tell against that hypothesis. Whatever the case, the fact that there were large creatures we call dinosaurs and that we must accept that they once existed remains on account of the continuing "effects" of their existence (namely fossils, and so forth).

In the case of the historical Jesus, the continuing "historical effects" are (primarily) the canonical gospels, other writings in the New Testament, as well as some other non-canonical Christian and non-Christian writings. These derive from the testimony of human beings (unlike the "historical effects" of the Big Bang or the dinosaurs). So, to a large extent, our knowledge of the historical Jesus, and our determination of his historical/historic significance, depends upon our trust or otherwise in the human witnesses. Artefacts, and archaeological material, may help us fill out, confirm or disconfirm that witness. But, in the end, it comes down to trust: not necessarily blind trust (the witnesses must be the subject of critical examination). A form of scepticism has arisen since Reimarus that has been given critical tools in the form of the criteria of authenticity that has attempted to prise a historical Jesus out of the accounts handed down by Christian tradition. This has given us, not necessarily the historical Jesus who lived, nor necessarily a Jesus understood in his historical significance, but a Jesus (or I should say, Jesuses) of scholarly reconstruction.[185] Faith, *pace* Theissen, is tentative, not based on secure historical facts but trust in witnesses, and trust that their determination of the historical significance of the Jesus they witness to seems plausible in the light of the evidence.

ENDNOTES

1. Albert Schweitzer, *The Quest of the Historical Jesus*. First complete edition edited by John Bowden (Minneapolis: Fortress, 2001). This is based on the (revised) 1913 German edition. The first German edition (from which an English translation was made by W. Montgomery, and published in 1910) was published in 1906 with the title, *Von Reimarus zu Wrede: Eine Geschichte der Leben-Jesu-Forschung* ("From Reimarus to Wrede: A history [or story?] of the Life-of-Jesus Research"). The full title of Montgomery's translated English volume was *The Quest of the Historical Jesus: A Critical Study of Its Progress from Reimarus to Wrede*.
2. The interrelationship between the first three gospels (Matthew, Mark and Luke) is called the Synoptic Problem, in that these gospels may be compared, side-by-side as it were, to study their similarities and differences. You may read about these issues in any good New Testament Introduction.
3. Sir Edwyn Hoskyns and Noel Davey, *The Riddle of the New Testament* (London: Faber and Faber, 1958).
4. Hoskyns and Davey, *Riddle*, 12.
5. Josephus, *Jewish Antiquities*, 18.63; see *The New Complete Works of Josephus*, translated by William Whiston; revised and expanded edition (Grand Rapids: Kregel, 1999), 590 (noted here as Book 18, Chapter 3.3).
6. Joachim Gnilka, *Jesus of Nazareth: Message and History* (translated by Siegfried S. Schatzmann. Peabody, Mass: Hendrickson, 1997), 319. See also Gerd Theissen and Annette Merz, *The Historical Jesus: A Comprehensive Guide* (translated by John Bowden. Minneapolis: Fortress, 1998), 503–4.
7. The development of "criteria of authenticity" is one such outcome (these are increasingly coming under criticism, and discarded as unfit for purpose); one might also think that the plethora of "historical Jesuses" is another, but I personally consider different reconstructions of Jesus are simply part of the process of historical reconstruction. One cannot expect to find *the* historical Jesus, one can only determine which historical reconstruction of Jesus seems the most plausible.

8. All scriptural quotations, unless otherwise noted, are from the New Revised Standard Version (NRSV) of the Bible (Anglicized Edition).
9. See Mary Louise Pratt, *Toward a Speech Act Theory of Literary Discourse* (Bloomington: Indiana University Press, 1977), pp. 81–91, especially p. 82 for the appropriateness conditions of statements, the second of which is "[the] speaker has evidence for the truth of *p* (or reasons for believing *p*)". Thus Paul is laying out the evidence.
10. See further Grant R. Osborne, "Jesus' Empty Tomb and His Appearance in Jerusalem", in *Key Events in the Life of the Historical Jesus: A Collaborative Exploration of Context and Coherence*, edited by Darrell L. Bock and Robert L. Webb (Grand Rapids: Eerdmans, 2010), 775–823, especially pp. 776–782.
11. See H. S. Reimarus, "Concerning the Intention of Jesus and His Teaching" in *Reimarus Fragments*, edited by Charles H. Talbert (London: SCM, 1971), 243–250.
12. Reimarus himself acknowledges this: the disciples are initially afraid and anxious that they will fall foul of the authorities. He maintains that they remain fearful and disoriented for some time after Jesus's death (see *Reimarus Fragments*, 244). Nonetheless, sometime within twenty-four hours (before decay set in), they decide to steal Jesus's body and come up with the idea of his resurrection (see *Reimarus Fragments*, 249).
13. John Dominic Crossan, *The Historical Jesus: The Life of a Mediterranean Jewish Peasant* (New York: HarperCollins, 1991), xxxii–xxxiii. Crossan speaks about the "complete avoidance" of any unit, like the Good Samaritan parable, that is singularly attested. He uses sigla to show what he considers from Jesus (+ = "originally from Jesus) and (- = not Jesus), and in his Inventory of units, he gives the parable a minus (-) sign (Appendix 1; 499). See John P. Meier, *A Marginal Jew: Rethinking the Historical Jesus. Volume V Probing the Authenticity of the Parables* (New Haven: Yale University Press, 2016), 199–209.
14. For instance, Luke probably created the Parable of the Good Samaritan (so Meier). If I was to look for someone other than Jesus as a great teller (or creator) parables, I also would look to Luke.
15. Markus Bockmuehl, "Resurrection", in *The Cambridge Companion to Jesus*, edited by Markus Bockmuehl (Cambridge: Cambridge University Press, 2001), 103.
16. The second option does not require a bodily resurrection. Rather, Jesus is raised "to the right hand of God" (see such texts as 1 Peter 1:21, 22; Acts 3:13; 5:30, 31; Ephesians 1:19, 20): God exalts Jesus, after his death, to God's right hand, and the early Christians become assured of this fact, perhaps in some cases by a vision of the resurrected Lord Jesus. The question that arises is why would the early Christians need subsequently to invent stories of a bodily resurrection, unnecessary in the case of Jews, and a foolish notion in the case of Gentiles?

17. My reading suggests that historical Jesus scholars refer to the resurrection in one of two ways: either it is called "the Easter event", or "the Easter experience".
18. Larry W. Hurtado, *How on Earth Did Jesus Become a God? Historical Questions about Earliest Devotion to Jesus* (Grand Rapids: Eerdmans, 2005).
19. See here N.T. Wright, *The Resurrection of the Son of God* (Minneapolis: Fortress Press, 2003), who lays out the arguments in detail, and show how the (orthodox) early Christian position offers the "best" explanation of the data.
20. Dale C. Allison, *Resurrecting Jesus: The Earliest Christian Tradition and Its Interpreters* (London/New York: T & T Clark International, 2005), 344–350, warns against arguing that the orthodox Christian understanding of the resurrection makes the best and most reasonable explanation of the historical data. He critiques N.T. Wright in particular in this regard [see N.T. Wright, *The Resurrection of the Son of God* (Minneapolis: Fortress, 2003)]. He argues, fairly, that we do not approach historical reconstruction from a "neutral standpoint" but rather "how we construe the data depends upon our worldview" (346). He claims that "James Anthony Froude, the nineteenth-century essayist and historian, got it just right: 'Of evidence for the resurrection in the common sense of the word, there may be enough to show that something extraordinary occurred; but not enough...to produce any absolute and unhesitating conviction; and inasmuch as the resurrection is the keystone of Christianity, the belief in it must be something far different from that suspended judgment in which history alone would leave us." (348; citing James Anthony Froude, *Short Studies on Great Subjects* [New York: Dutton, 1964], 211–12). I think, however, that there must be an argument that a theological explanation for something that is claimed to have happened in history, must not thereby be excluded as also a form of historical explanation. My objection is against the tendency to relegate matters to "theology" and, thereby, imply, or even suggest outright, that it is therefore not "history". A theologically described datum may also be an historical datum, and indeed, must if the Christian belief that God is involved in history has any weight. It is because this cannot be a universally held position that can be subscribed to by all historians, that it cannot be considered as more than one interpretation alongside others.
21. See John P. Meier, *A Marginal Jew*. Vol. 1, 41, 140, 167; Helen K. Bond, *The Historical Jesus: A Guide for the Perplexed* (London: T & T Clark International, 2012), 52.
22. See comments by N.T. Wright, *Jesus and the Victory of God* (London: SPCK, 1996), xvi. J. P. Meier, *A Marginal Jew*. Vol. 1, 45; James D. G. Dunn, *Christianity in the Making, Volume 1: Jesus Remembered* (Grand Rapids: Eerdmans, 2003), p. 165, states that "[F.C.] Baur's dismissal of John's Gospel as a historical source held increasingly undisputed sway for about a hundred years." An interest group within the Society of Biblical Literature, "The John, Jesus,

and History Group", has done much work to rehabilitate the Gospel as an historical source.

23. This is such a large issue that I cannot cover it here, but have attempted a (still inadequately brief) discussion in the Appendix. It might be noted here, however, that the criteria of authenticity have come under a lot of scrutiny and criticism in recent years; they are increasingly being abandoned as useful tools for historical reconstruction.

24. Again, even a fairly cursory examination of the scholarship will alert a reader to the fact that this is a large and complex issue. There are scholars who maintain that Luke derives his "Q" material from Matthew (and some have it the other way around). Even to say that "Q" represents material found in Matthew and Luke, but not in Mark, has to be nuanced, as scholars speak of overlaps between Mark and Q.

25. See James D. G. Dunn, *A New Perspective on Jesus: What the Quest for the Historical Jesus Missed* (Grand Rapids: Baker Academic, 2005), and *Jesus Remembered*, Christianity in the Making, Volume 1 (Grand Rapids: Eerdmans, 2003), see especially chapter eight.

26. Dunn writes of "re-envisaging the early transmission of the Jesus tradition" (*New Perspective*, 101); and "reconceptualising the traditioning process" (*Jesus Remembered*, 334). See also his demurral about the possibility of "producing a knockdown argument" (*New Perspective*, 101), and comments regarding retrieving an initial composition of Q from redactions of it, or the "unavoidably speculative" nature of sequencing Mark's arrangement of "groupings already familiar in the oral traditioning process" (*Jesus Remembered*, 247). The reconstructive process may also be surmised from comments such as "we can envisage" (239); "we may imagine" (340); or "Jesus would have taught [the disciples when he sent them out on mission] what to say" (243). I do not wish to dismiss Dunn's arguments, nor his reconstruction of the oral traditioning process, which is cogent and, I think, the best hypothesis put forward. My comments are simply to highlight that the historical task in reconstructive: the period being examined is a dark tunnel, and the data available tricky to use.

27. Again, note the comment by Dunn on the difficulty in defining the scope and limits of Q, "since wherever Matthew or Luke decided not to use 'Q', we do not have 'Q'!" (*New Perpective*, 122). In his discussion on the fact that the Synoptic Evangelists used material already circulating orally, so that "when the Synoptic Gospels were first received by various churches, these churches *already* possessed (in communal oral memory or in written form) their own versions of much of the material. They would be able to compare the Evangelist's version ...with their own versions" (*Jesus Remembered*, 250, emphasis original). Perhaps; and granted also that oral tradition continued to circulated alongside of, and after the production of the gospels. However, my point here is, is that *we* now only have access to the written gospels.

28. Derek Tovey, *Jesus, Story of God: John's Story of Jesus* (Hindmarsh: ATF Press, 2007), and *Read Mark and Learn: Following Mark's Jesus* (Eugene, Oreg: Wipf & Stock, 2014).
29. In narrative terms, I prefer to speak of "the implied author" rather than the evangelist. The implied author is the profile of the real author (the evangelist) that has been embedded in the narrative, and which profile the reader discerns in reading the narrative.
30. *The Kalevala: An Epic Poem After Oral Tradition by Elias Lönnrot.* Translated from the Finnish with an Introduction and Notes by Keith Bosley (The World's Classics; Oxford: Oxford University Press, 1989), xxvi. In fact, this epic in its current form was brought together in the nineteenth century by Elias Lönnrot, working with traditional singers. As Bosley shows, it was Lönnrot who gave *The Kalevala* its shape and character (see xxviii–xxxiv). He writes: "Lönnrot did his work so well that some people thought he had restored a lost epic from its scattered fragments: that is at least a tribute to his literary sense" (xxxi). On the gospel creation, note Harry Emerson Fosdick, *The Man from Nazareth* (London: SCM, 1950), 23; and also James D.G. Dunn, *The Oral Gospel Tradition* (Grand Rapids: Eerdmans, 2013), 1.
31. Albert B. Lord, *The Singer of Tales*. Harvard Studies in Comparative Literature (Cambridge, Mass: Harvard University Press, 1960), 4.
32. Lord, *Singer*, 13.
33. Lord, *Singer*, 101–102.
34. "Fragments of Papias" in *The Apostolic Fathers: Greek Texts and English Translations,* edited and translated by Michael W. Holmes, 3rd edition (Grand Rapids: Baker Academic, 2007), 739–41; fragments 15, 16. Note that though I refer to "the writings of Papias", we do not have these, except as are found quoted in the writings of others, in this case in Eusebius's *Ecclesiastical History,* see Book III, xxxix, 15, 16
35. On this see, Jonathan Bernier, *Rethinking the Dates of the New Testament: The Evidence for Early Composition* (Grand Rapids: Baker Academic, 2022), 73–77; Richard Bauckham, *Jesus and the Eyewitnesses: The Gospels as Eyewitness Testimony* (Grand Rapids: Eerdmans, 2006), 205–221. Chapter Two deals with Papias's relationship to the eyewitnesses generally. Irenaeus (*Against Heresies* 3.1.1) also mentions that Mark is Peter's disciple and "interpreter", but he may well be dependent upon Papias for this description (see Adela Yarbro Collins, *Mark.* Hermeneia (Minneapolis: Fortress, 2007), 7.
36. See here, Jonathan Bernier, *The Quest for the Historical Jesus After the Demise of Authenticity: Toward a Critical Realist Philosophy of History in Jesus Studies.* LNTS 540 (London: Bloomsbury, 2016), 149–50. Bernier draws attention to the work of Gerhardsson, *Memory and Manuscript*, 234–45 (fn. 58).
37. See J.A.T. Robinson's reflections on Papias's testimony in *Redating the New Testament* (London: SCM, 1976), 95–98. I should note that this compilation

of oracles by Matthew does not mean that some of the material in Matthew has been translated from this "document" (if such it was). The Gospel of Matthew is written in Greek, and is of such a character that it is not likely to depend upon a translation from Hebrew. However, Papias's comment about others "interpreting" the oracles as best they could, may have some germ of a suggestion as to the relationship between a collection of oracles in Hebrew and Matthew's Gospel. Bernier, *Quest*, 143-44, briefly summarises "two basic schools of interpretation" regarding Papias's comment about Matthew arranging the oracles "in a Hebraic language/dialect": "it either refers to a "Hebraic language", perhaps Aramaic or Hebrew; or it refers to Greek written in a 'Hebraic style.'" M. Hengel, *The Four Gospels and the One Gospel of Jesus Christ* (translated by John Bowden; London: SCM, 2000), conjectures that Matthew may have produced a collection of saying of Jesus in Aramaic, which were, perhaps, subsequently incorporated into the (Greek) Gospel of Matthew, or rather "Matthew", the anonymous author of the Gospel (who attributed the Gospel to the disciple) incorporated the Aramaic source (or sources) into his Gospel (see 177-78, 205).

38. See here Holmes, "Fragments of Papias", 735; fragment 3. Papias is stating how he has written about what he has learned from "the elders", and then goes on to say: "And if by chance someone who had been a follower of the elders should come my way, I inquired about the words of the elders–what Andrew or Peter said, or Philip or Thomas or James or John or Matthew or any other of the Lord's disciples, and whatever Aristion and the elder John, the Lord's disciples, were saying. For I did not think that information from books would profit me as much as information from a living and abiding voice." See Dunn, *Jesus Remembered*, 242-43, for a comment about the importance of individual bearers of Jesus tradition. I should note that Holmes himself sees Papias's testimony as valuable for highlighting the continuing importance of oral tradition even after the gospels were written (see p. 723).

39. J.A.T Robinson raised this question in the 1970s in *Redating the New Testament*, and Jonathan Bernier has recently revived and extended the discussion in his *Rethinking the Dates of the New Testament*. Perhaps a sea-change in the consensus, as periodically happens in biblical scholarship, is about to occur?

40. See, however, the Appendix.

41. R.G. Collingwood, *The Idea of History*. (Revised Edition; Oxford: Oxford University Press, 1994), 231-249, especially 241, 245.

42. See E. H. Carr, *What is History?* (Harmondsworth: Penguin, 1964), 10. G.R. Elton, *The Practice of History* (London: Collins, 1969), 75-78, takes Carr to task, unfairly I think, accusing him of "extreme relativism" and denying that there can be such a thing as an "historical fact" (only a "fact of history" created by the historian). But Elton misreads Carr; see what Carr writes on pp. 26-27. And the examples Elton gives really amount to the type of "facts" that might appear in a chronicle i.e. *that* a man died, *that* e.g. William the Conqueror

invaded Britain. These "facts" need to be interpreted: what did they mean, why did they happen? Elton himself writes on William the Conqueror's invasion: "We may not know precisely why William the Conqueror decided to invade England; we do know that he did invade and had a reason for doing so. We may argue over his invasion and its motive; we cannot argue them away" (74). But isn't it precisely the why and the reason William the Conqueror invaded England that is the stuff of history? (I doubt whether Carr would "argue away" *that* the invasion happened).

43. John Dominic Crossan, *The Historical Jesus: The Life of a Mediterranean Jewish Peasant* (New York: HarperCollins, 1991), xxvii.
44. See W.B. Gallie, *Philosophy and the Historical Understanding.* (Second Edition; New York: Schocken Books, 1964), chapters two and three for a full account of his argument. I have an abbreviated summary in my *Narrative Art and Act in the Fourth Gospel* (Sheffield: Sheffield Academic Press, 1997), 203–205; see also *Jesus: Story of God*, 160–1. As far as I am aware, "followable story" is my term, derived from his work: Gallie himself refers to Collingwood saying that a historian "seeks to construct a 'coherent picture'" [and goes on] "(we should prefer to say, to construct a 'followable narrative')", p.56.
45. Gallie, *Philosophy*, 67.
46. Bernier, *Quest*, 162.
47. Bernier, *Quest*, 73–75, on the "Bethany/Bethphage Complex", and for a supposition that he recruited supporters in this region, see 83. We might even add "an unknown woman who anointed Jesus in the house of Simon the leper" (Matt 26:6–13//Mark 14:3–9, but cf. John 12:1–8). Jesus evidently made Bethany a base, (see Mark 11:11), so presumably had supporters there with whom he could stay.
48. Bernier, *Quest*, 76–81.
49. Bernier, *Quest*, 81–83, specifically 83.
50. Gallie, *Philosophy*, 89.
51. E.P. Sanders, *The Historical Figure of Jesus* (London: Penguin Books, 1993).
52. Sanders, *Historical Figure*, 10–11. Cf. his *Jesus and Judaism* (London: SCM, 1985), 11, where the phrase "almost indisputable facts" is used, but where a shorter list is provided.
53. John P. Meier, *A Marginal Jew: Rethinking the Historical Jesus.* Volumes 1–5; The Anchor (Yale) Bible Reference Library (New York: Doubleday/New Haven: Yale University Press, 1991–2016).
54. In Sanders case, the link with the movement that remained is brought out more strongly in his *Jesus and Judaism*.
55. When I use the term "event" it stands for a discrete historical event, or a large complex of individual historical events brought under the conspectus of one examination of those events: hence, it may be an account of, say, D-Day, or an account of World War II as a whole. The data that supplies material for

a reconstruction may be documents of various kinds, archaeological artefacts, ruins, buildings, and even geographical or topographical features. In terms of contemporary history, data may now also include video and film material, and oral eyewitness accounts.

56. There is debate over whether or not this letter can be attributed to the apostle Peter. But, even if it cannot, it expresses, no doubt, a sentiment with which Peter, and all eyewitnesses to Jesus would concur.
57. James D. G. Dunn, *New Perspective*, 33. I am not sufficiently competent as a reader of German to know whether the distinction between *Geschichte* and *Historie* is useful or helpful, as my limited grasp of some of the discussions on these terms suggest to me that the subtleties of various meanings that attach to them make use of them problematic. However, I believe that Dunn's statement above is a helpful encapsulation of the issue of *historical significance*, or, if you like, the *historic* meaning of Jesus.
58. James D. G. Dunn, *A New Perspective on Jesus*, 33.
59. N.A. Dahl, "Kergyma and History", in *In Search of the Historical Jesus*, edited by Harvey K. McArthur (London: SPCK, 1970), 133.
60. On this see Murray A. Rae, *History and Hermeneutics* (London: T & T Clark, 2005), 49, who writes that "the Bible is a theological account of history." Chapter Two of this book is a useful and important survey of various forms of (theological) history since Kähler.
61. See e.g. N. T. Wright, *The Resurrection of the Son of God*, 716–718. The following chapter lays out the historic significance of Jesus, in Wright's view, in the light of Jesus's resurrection.
62. See Dale Allison, *Resurrecting Jesus*, 344-350.
63. This is too large a topic to address here. An easy entry into some of the issues and approaches is Bart D. Ehrman, *How Jesus Became God: The Exaltation of a Jewish Preacher from Galilee* (New York: HarperCollins, 2014. For a response to Ehrman's arguments, see Michael F. Bird, Craig A. Evans, Simon J. Gathercole, Charles H. Hill and Chris Tilling, *How God Became Jesus: The Real Origins of Belief in Jesus' Divine Nature–A Response to Bart Ehrman* (Grand Rapids: Zondervan, 2014). Dag Oistein Endsjo, *Greek Resurrection Beliefs and the Success of Christianity* (New York: Palgrave MacMillan, 2009), takes a slightly different tack. It was the claim for bodily resurrection of Jesus that attracted them to Christianity. "...Greeks became Christians partly *because* of the Christian belief in the resurrection of the flesh" (x). Endsjo does affirm that Christian belief in the resurrection is rooted in Jewish thinking, and does admit that the nature of the beliefs were different from pagan beliefs. His argument may show how Christian beliefs were able to appeal to Greek, or pagan beliefs, and how these could provide a bridge to understanding the Christian beliefs. But he does not really address the question of why the Christian beliefs should have arisen, nor why they developed as they did so rapidly.

64. Larry W. Hurtado, *How on Earth Did Jesus Become God? Historical Questions about Earliest Devotion to Jesus* (Grand Rapids: Eerdmans, 2005), 4.
65. Larry W. Hurtado, *At the Origins of Christian Worship: The Context and Character of Earliest Christian Devotion* (Carlisle: Paternoster, 1999/Grand Rapids: Eerdmans, 2000), 97 (italics original). This book provides a good entrée into Hurtado's argument. See also his *One God, One Lord: Early Christian Devotion and Ancient Jewish Monotheism* (Philadelphia: Fortress, 1988; and *Lord Jesus Christ: Devotion to Jesus in Earliest Christianity* (Grand Rapids: Eerdmans, 2003). James D. G. Dunn, *Did the First Christian Worship Jesus? The New Testament Evidence* (London: SPCK/Louisville, KY: Westminster John Knox, 2010) takes issue with Hurtado, arguing that the earliest Christians showed more reserve in their worship. They did not worship Jesus as such, but worshiped God in and through Jesus, and any devotion given to Jesus was always in the context of worship ultimately offered to the glory of God the Father (on this see p.146, and his conclusion, pp. 147–151). I think, however, that his argument comes down to such fine distinctions that he comes almost to the same place as Hurtado.
66. On this see *Lord Jesus Christ*, 64–74, especially, 71–72; and *One God, One Lord*, 117–22.
67. Scholars often assume that Paul is referring to his vision of Jesus on the Damascus Road (see Acts 9:3–5; 22:6–11; 26:13–16). In 2 Corinthians 12:1, Paul writes about "visions and revelations of the Lord", but goes on to speak about a particular experience that does not seem to include an appearance of the Risen Lord Jesus.
68. "Last of all, as to one untimely born, he appeared also to me." (1 Cor. 15:8). Scholars debate the meaning of this verse, and especially the reference to being "untimely born", a phrase that generally applied to a premature birth, either by abortion or miscarriage, or naturally. A consensus seems to be that it may be a derogatory reference, which Paul either picks up from some opponents and applies against himself, or uses it of himself, to make the point that although he might be regarded as a freak, or a "monster" because of his pre-Christian behaviour towards Christians, he nevertheless ranks amongst the apostles as one who has "seen the Lord" (cf. 1 Cor. 9:1).
69. "But when God, who set me apart before I was born and called me through his grace, was pleased to reveal his Son to me,..." (Gal.1:15–16a; see the marginal, or footnote, reading "in me"; the Greek phrase can be translated either way).
70. Richard B. Hays, *First Corinthians*. Interpretation: A Bible Commentary for Teaching and Preaching (Louisville: John Knox, 1997), 257.
71. The language of "pre-Easter" and "post-Easter" Jesus is that used by Marcus Borg; see his *Meeting Jesus Again for the First Time* (New York: HarperCollins, 1995), 15–16. This has the advantage (as opposed to "Jesus of History" and "Christ of Faith" language) of highlighting that the same historical person is in

view. What is under debate is how much the proclaimed "post-Easter" Jesus of the early church is a distorted (or faith-inspired) picture of the pre-Easter Jesus; and how the two should relate to one another.

72. Luke 13:29 (possibly "the last" Jesus had in mind were non-Jews); the fact that Jesus considers that Tyre and Sidon would have repented more readily than Chorazin and Bethsaida are prepared to, suggests that he saw them as falling within the realm of God's acceptance, and capable of being part of God's kingdom (see Luke 10:13). Some of the parables of judgment, e.g. the parable of the weeds among the weeds (Matt 13:24–30, 36–43); the parable of the dragnet (Matt 13:47–50)–with their suggestion of the indiscriminate nature of the harvesting, and catch–imply a universal note to the teaching about the kingdom.

73. See Pss 24:7–10; 93:1–2; 96:10; 97:1; 99:1, 4; Isa. 6:5; 43:15; Jer. 8:19; 10:6, 7, 10; 1 Sam. 8:7 (one side of the debate over kingship, and whether Israel should have a king, was that as God was their king, no earthly king should be necessary). It is likely that references to God as "shepherd" of Israel in the Old Testament, also carried the connotation of kingship.

74. Of course, the Old Testament also affirmed that "the earth is the Lord's" (Ps. 24:1), and that God ruled over all the earth (Ps. 47:2, 7; Josh. 3:13). Throughout the Old Testament, there runs a thread that affirms that it is God who is the king over all.

75. Matthew has, of course, arranged this teaching to suit his narrative purpose. Jesus is being presented as a "new Moses" who is providing his listeners with an understanding of what it means to be truly members of God's kingdom.

76. For scholars who look for the "authentic words" of Jesus, I suggest that this Jesus tradition is unlikely to have been created by the early church. The material comes from "Q" tradition, and the question of tithing various herbs was probably not an issue for their Christian audience.

77. Ironically, the Jesus Seminar apparently rejected Matt 23:23 as an inauthentic Jesus saying (although "not alien to [his] sentiments"), because it "expresses a common prophetic criticism, like the one stated in Mic 6:8"; see *The Five Gospels: The Search for the Authentic Words of Jesus.* New Translation and Commentary by Robert W. Funk, Roy W. Hoover, and the Jesus Seminar (New York: Polebridge/Macmillan, 1993), 242.

78. This follows a parable about God's vineyard yielding "wild grapes" (Isa 5:1–7, which concludes by stating that the vineyard is "the house of Judah", in which God expected justice, but found only bloodshed, and looked for righteousness but heard only "a cry" (presumably a cry against injustice). We might recall that Jesus used the metaphor of a vineyard to accuse the Jewish authorities of rejecting God's prophets, and finally God's beloved son (Mark 12:1–12//Luke 20:9–16//Matt. 21:33–44 (here Jesus speaks of the kingdom of God being taken away and given to those who produce "the fruits of the kingdom").

79. This description of Jesus's intentions and aims is provided by E.P. Sanders, *Jesus and Judaism*, 118, 323; see also Marcus Borg, *Jesus, A New Vision* (London: SPCK, 1993), 125–26.
80. Possibly this might extend to the end of the chapter (v. 18), but the conclusion of the final verse suggests that this section might be taken as a universal "day of wrath".
81. Though possibly exile is the likely outcome (Amos 5:27).
82. Mic 3:4 extends the picture to include a bucolic scene of everyone sitting under their own vine, or fig trees, unafraid.
83. This might be extended through Joel 2:30–3:3, which has an apocalyptic tone, and extends judgment universally.
84. Note here it is a remnant ("the survivors of Israel") who are led out by the Lord, with their king passing out before them (like a shepherd leading his sheep?).
85. Eric Meyers, "Zechariah" in *The New Interpreter's Study Bible*, edited by Walter J. Harrelson, et.al. (Nashville: Abingdon, 2003), 1342, sees this passage as a "messianic oracle", and links it with Zech 4:6b–10a.
86. Possibly a conflation of Mal 3:1 and Exod 23:20. Mark 1:3//Matt 3:3//Luke 3:4 quote Isaiah 40:3.
87. Warren Carter, "Matthew" in *The New Interpreter's Study Bible*, 1765, writes: "Jesus uses Isaiah's visions of God's liberating empire (Isa 26:19; 29:18-19; 35:5-6; 42:7; 61:1) to sum up his merciful mission among the marginalized."
88. John P. Meier, *A Marginal Jew: Rethinking the Historical Jesus. Volume V: Probing the Authenticity of the Parables* (New Haven: Yale University Press, 2016), 240–53. Meier, however, considers Mark 12:9–11 as later additions by the early church (252).
89. Matt 22:41; cf. Luke 20:41, where one might assume it is the Sadducees, cf. 20:27, 34; Mark 12:35, where it appears that the question is directed at "the large crowd listening to him".
90. See below pp. 65–66.
91. Meier, *A Marginal Jew*, Vol. 5, 48, 190–91.
92. Particularly, I would argue, when the nature of the parable as "undecided" is determined on the dubious grounds of the criteria of authenticity.
93. See Meier, *Marginal Jew*, Vol. 5, 200, 207 (where Meier describes the author of the parable as "Luke the artist"), 209. Meier does not go as far as attributing all the "L" parables to Luke, but some other "L" parables may come from Luke's hand.
94. One of the problems with Form Criticism was that scholars could not agree on what the sociological (or ecclesiastical) purposes of the created material were. The approach of other scholars appears to be simply to say "this is not Jesus, this is a creation of the early church" and to leave it at that.
95. Some commentators make this link, as Mark 4:26–29 is a kingdom parable relating to the growth of the kingdom (see e.g. Robert A. Guelich, *Mark*

1–8:26. Word Biblical Commentary 34A (Nashville: Thomas Nelson, 1989), 206. It has been argued that the explanation (Mark 4:14–20) is a creation of the early church. In that case, we cannot be sure what Jesus meant by the parable itself. It is certainly the case that Mark has carefully placed this parable, not long after the choice of the twelve disciples (Mark 3:13–19) and some pointed comments that those who are truly Jesus's family are those who do the will of God (Mark 3:31–35), as an introduction to the teaching of Jesus and how it should be received. Mark, I think, intends not only the explanation, but two little sayings that follow to apply to the theme of "paying attention to what you hear" (cf. Mark 4:24). The whole chapter is carefully woven together to raise the issue not only of the nature and style of Jesus's teaching (about the kingdom, which is "mystery" to those "outside") but how one should receive it and the effort required to grasp hold of it (see Mark 4:33, 34). I have explored this in more depth in my *Read Mark and Learn,* 70–74.

96. In C.H. Dodd's memorable phrase. See C.H. Dodd, *The Parables of the Kingdom* (Glasgow: Collins/Fount Paperbacks, 1978), 16. Dodd's definition of a parable is worth quoting in full: "At its simplest the parable is a metaphor or simile drawn from nature or common life, arresting the hearer by its vividness or strangeness, and leaving the mind in sufficient doubt about its precise application to tease it into active thought."
97. See Geza Vermes, *Jesus the Jew* (London: Collins, 1973), Chapter Three. See also his *Jesus in his Jewish Context* (London: SCM, 2003), 4–10.
98. John P. Meier, *A Marginal Jew: Rethinking the Historical Jesus: Volume Two: Mentor, Message, and Miracles.* The Anchor Yale Reference Library. (New York: Doubleday, 1994), devotes a chapter (17) to discussing the issue of the modern historian's approach to miracles.
99. Jesus is later said to be "on the beach" (21:4) and here the preposition might be *epi* (on), although there is a textual issue here, as some manuscripts read *eis* (towards, to).
100. Guelich, *Mark 1–8:26,* 350
101. I have made this suggestion in *Read Mark and Learn,* 50, fn 18, see 41–50 where I examine how Mark develops the eucharistic theme under a "one loaf" motif.
102. Tovey, *Read Mark and Learn,* 82–85.
103. John P. Meier, *A Marginal Jew. Volume Two,* finds the miracle tradition to be well supported by two of the criteria of authenticity (multiple attestation, and coherence). So he affirms "that Jesus performed extraordinary deeds deemed by himself and others to be miracles" as a historical fact (630). See pp. 969–70 for his summary of which miracles (or types of miracles) are most likely to be authentic to Jesus.
104. *The New Complete Works of Josephus.* Translated by William Whiston. Revised and Expanded Edition (Grand Rapids: Kregel, 1999), 590. See comment by John P. Meier on this testimony in *A Marginal Jew. Volume Two,* 592–93.

105. Rudolf Bultmann, *History of the Synoptic Tradition*, Translated by John Marsh (Peabody/Oxford: Hendrickson/Basil Blackwell, 1963), 261-62 (quotation on p. 262).
106. Brent Kinman, "Jesus' Royal Entry into Jerusalem" in *Key Events in the Life of the Historical Jesus: A Collaborative Exploration of Context and Coherence*, edited by Darrell L. Bock and Robert L. Webb (Grand Rapids: Eerdmans, 2010), 420. See this whole chapter for a cogent argument for the historicity of this incident.
107. John 2:13 and John 6:4 suggest that there were two Passovers prior to the Passover mentioned in 12:1.
108. Literary critics state that discourse time (that is the amount of story that elapses between time references) provides a reader also with a sense of the progress of chronological time. In that case, in both Matthew and Luke (to a lesser extent Mark) the amount of discourse time between the story of the "triumphal entry" and the time note "two days" before the Passover, might give the sense of a long elapse of time.
109. The chronological considerations here also raise the question of the length of Jesus's ministry. Was it about two-and-a-half years to three years, as John's Gospel seems to suggest, or anything from a few months to a year, as some scholars suggest Mark's Gospel indicates? On this, see John P. Meier, *A Marginal Jew: Rethinking the Historical Jesus. Volume One: The Roots of the Problem and the Person.* The Anchor Bible Reference Library (New York: Doubleday, 1991), 403–06. Meier argues that the Synoptic accounts allow for a longer ministry than might appear. He opts for a ministry of two years and a couple of months. Cf. Sanders, *Historical Figure*, 13; Dunn, *Jesus Remembered*, 312.
110. It is possible that John's reference to the Passover ought to be taken as a literary device, rather than a chronological marker. In other words, the focus of John's Gospel is on *the* Passover at which Jesus was crucified. The Gospel narrative circles around this theme of Passover so that the phrase "the Passover of the Jews was near" (2:13; 6:4) is a thematic marker, rather like a story of a significant event stating periodically, "the Big Day was drawing nearer". I make this suggestion in my book, *Jesus: Story of God*, 72–73. Admittedly, a narrative approach (and many readers' assumptions) would generally hold that a series of temporal markers throughout a narrative indicates the (forward) passage of time.
111. E.P. Sanders, *Historical Figure*, 260–62, articulates this view well, and may be taken as representative of this position. He thinks that Jesus expected God to provide "a new and perfect Temple" in the coming age (261). See also his *Jesus and Judaism*, Chapter One.
112. Matthew certainly believed that Jesus's ministry was solely directed at Israel (see Matt 10:5, 6; 15:24).
113. Isaiah 2:2–4; 56:6, 7; 66:18–20, cf. Zephaniah 9, 10; Zechariah 8:20–23; 14:16–21.

114. On John's Gospel's use of Ps 69:9 (and other possible scriptural associations in this pericope) see Andreas J. Köstenberger, "John", in *Commentary on the New Testament Use of the Old Testament*, edited by G.K. Beale and D. A. Carson (Grand Rapids: Baker Academic, 2007), 431–34; see esp. 433 on Zech. 14:21.
115. Köstenberger, "John", 433.
116. Rudolf Bultmann, *Theology of the New Testament*. Volume 1. Translated by Kendrick Grobel (New York: Charles Scribner's Sons, 1951), 33: "He who formerly had been the *bearer* of the message was draw into it and became its essential *content. The proclaimer became the proclaimed–*" (italics original).
117. Possibly the tradition is only the "creedal" statement found in vv. 3–4: but logically it would seem that the verses detailing the various people to whom the Risen Jesus appeared is part of what was "handed on" to Paul. After all, apart from his reference to Christ's appearance to him (v. 8), he must have received the information about the other appearances from others.
118. J. Paul Sampley, "I Corinthians" in *The New Interpreter's Bible* states in a note on 11:23: "*From the Lord* Paul is crediting Jesus' power through the church's tradition. *Handed on* is a technical term for the transmission of tradition (11:2)" (2052).
119. A date anywhere between 53 to 55 CE would seem to be the general consensus.
120. The Corinthian Christians are gathering to eat a shared meal, in the course of which they will remember the death of Jesus. But the fact that some eat before others arrive, and one goes hungry while another gets drunk, and that Paul later (v. 33) enjoins them to "wait for one another", suggests that a general, supposedly shared, meal is being held. The lack of thought for those who miss out (probably poorer members of the church) is a direct denial of the "self-giving" of Jesus, witnessed supremely in his death, the very thing their practice of the Lord's Supper is supposed to remember. This attitude and behaviour, Paul says, means that what they do, does not really constitute the Lord's Supper (v. 20) as it destroys the spirit of the remembrance.
121. This is the wording in Mark's Gospel. Matthew has, for the bread, "Take, eat; this is my body", while Luke has, "This is my body, which is given for you. Do this in remembrance of me." For the cup, Matthew gives Jesus's words as, "Drink of it, all of you; for this is my blood of the covenant, which is poured out for many for the forgiveness of sins"; Luke's version is, "This cup which is poured out for you is the new covenant in my blood". In 1 Cor. 11:24, 25, Paul gives Jesus's words as: "This is my body which is for you. Do this in remembrance of me" (for the bread), and "This cup is the new covenant in my blood. Do this, as often as you drink it, in remembrance of me" (for the cup). How these variations arose is impossible to determine. Perhaps different witnesses remembered the words differently; or, as is perhaps more likely, different traditions arose as the early Christians participated in a remembrance of the Lord's death in the Eucharistic meal.

122. N. Perrin, "Last Supper" in *Dictionary of Jesus and the Gospels*, edited by Joel B. Green et. al. Second Edition (Downers Grove: InterVarsity, 2013), 493. I am not sure whether the disciples understood Jesus's actions sufficiently well to be able to say that they "confessed" Jesus as Messiah by their eating and drinking. Full understanding only came after they had seen the Risen Jesus. However, this act made a very deep impression upon them, as it witnessed by the fact that the early church kept alive the tradition.
123. There is little point in trying to reconstruct what Jesus originally said. What we have in the gospels is a translation anyway, so we can never reconstruct exactly what was said.
124. The Greek form of the title here (*huios anthrōpou*) is different from that found in the gospels (except at John 5:27) where it is *ho huios tou anthrōpou*. In fact, in Revelation the phrase is "[one] like the Son of Man" (NRSV; the Greek is *homoion huion anthrōpou*). While the identification with the Danielic Son of Man is virtually certain in Revelation according to many scholars, they would maintain that the same cannot be said for all the Son of Man sayings in the gospels.
125. Is it significant that this use of the descriptor is by someone close to the time when Jesus was crucified, and when his use of the descriptor as a self-reference was still a fresh memory? As time went on, the memory of Jesus *using* this descriptor of himself remained (hence its use in the gospels), but the early Christians themselves tended to speak of Jesus in other ways, as "Messiah", "Lord" and "Son of God".
126. Bruce Chilton, "(The) Son of (the) Man, and Jesus" in *Authenticating the Words of Jesus*, edited by Bruce Chilton & Craig A. Evans (Leiden: Brill, 1999), writes: "They [the crowd] understand 'messiah' and they understand 'Son of Man,' and *for that reason* they do not understand the messianic Son of Man" (283, emphasis original). It is clear that the crowd understand Jesus to be speaking of the Messiah, so perhaps they do understand "Son of Man" to be a designation for the Messiah. However, I am not sure: it is clear that they understand Jesus to be linking his "lifting up" with the "hour" of the Son of Man, but perhaps they do not understand what Jesus means when he refers to the "Son of Man". They say, in effect, "We don't know what you mean by referring to the Son of Man, and who is he anyway?" Something about his use of the descriptor must suggest he links "Son of Man" with "Messiah", but the evangelist leaves this ambiguous: perhaps this catches the tenor of Jesus's use of the descriptor. Chilton's larger point that Jesus's use moves in the realm of poetry, so that he may be using the phrase in both a generic (referring to himself as a human being) and a messianic sense is worth noting.
127. Other instances of Group One sayings (referring to present activity or circumstances of Jesus's ministry) I would note are Luke 9:55 (a marginal reading, but expressing a sentiment similar to Luke 19:10); Luke 22:48, Jesus's words to

Judas as Judas betrays him with a kiss. Matt 13:37 is an explanation of the parable of the weeds among the wheat, in which Jesus is represented as identifying the Son of Man as the sower of the good seed; this is an interesting instance in that the explanation goes on to identify a future action of the Son of Man at the time of judgment (a Group Three statement, relating to the future Son of Man). Another interesting use of the descriptor, Son of Man, comes in Luke 24:7, where the angels' message to the women reminds them of Jesus prediction while still in Galilee, that "the Son of Man must be handed over to sinners…" Some further sayings, that I would place in Group Two (sayings about Jesus's death), include Mark 9:9//Matt 17:9, where Jesus enjoins silence upon Peter, James and John until after the Son of Man has risen from the dead (only Matthew has this in direct speech); and Mark 9:12//Matt 17:12, where Jesus asks why scripture should speak of suffering for the Son of Man (Mark) or reiterates that the Son of Man will suffer (Matt). Mark 10:45//Matt 20:28 provide a purpose for Jesus's death as "a ransom for many".

128. In Matthew's account the crowd "glorified God, who had given such authority to human beings" (Matt 9:8). John appears to use the descriptor, Son of Man, in contexts where he particularly wants to emphasise the humanness of Jesus.

129. Obviously, the instance of John 5:27 just given above, may also be (and perhaps more appropriately?) associated with Synoptic texts on the Son of Man's role as judge. This would be a further example that John, at least, associates the Son of Man with Jesus.

130. Mark adds "and the gospel". Matthew 16:24–28 speaks of the Son of Man rewarding everyone for what they have done, but again it is in the context of having spoken about a person's response to Jesus's call to discipleship.

131. Jesus's reply, "I am" (Greek: *egō eimi*) is reminiscent of the divine name spoken to Moses at the burning bush, in the Septuagint (LXX) it is rendered *egō eimi ho ōn*. See also Mark 6:50, where Jesus reassures the disciples when approaching them walking on the water by saying: "Take heart, it is I (Greek: *egō eimi*).

132. This is the case with other texts not mentioned above. For instance, Matt 10:23 comes in the context of Jesus sending the twelve out on mission, and where persecution will come on account of Jesus's name. The apocalyptic teaching in Matthew 24–25 where there are references to the Son of Man (Matt 24:22, 30, 37, 39, 44; 25:31) is introduced by a question from the disciples in which they say, "Tell us, when will this be, and what will be the sign of *your* coming and of the end of the age?" (Matt 24:3; note by the way how Jesus immediately warns against people coming *in his name*, claiming to be the Messiah).

133. Gerd Theissen, "From the Historical Jesus to the Kerygmatic Son of God: How Role Analysis Contributes to the Understanding of New Testament Christology" in *Jesus Research: New Methodologies and Perceptions,* edited by James H. Charlesworth (Grand Rapids: Eerdmans, 2014), 252; italics original. The opinion Theissen expresses here is his own, though his article stands as a

survey of the current scholarly thinking on the significance of the expression "Son of Man".

134. Adela Yarbro Collins, "Son of Man" in *The New Interpreter's Dictionary of the Bible*. Volume 5, edited by Katherine Doob Sakenfeld (Nashville: Abingdon, 2009), 344.
135. See e.g. Adela Yarbro Collins, *Mark: A Commentary*. Hermeneia (Minneapolis: Fortress, imprint of Augsburg Fortress, 2007), 600.
136. Collins, *Mark*, 189, 204–5, 402.
137. Barnabas Lindars, "Son of Man" in *A Dictionary of Biblical Interpretation*, edited by R. J. Coggins & J. L. Houlden (London/Philadelphia: SCM/Trinity Press International, 1990), 640.
138. Matthew Black, in a note appended to Appendix E in which Geza Vermes discusses the use of *bar enash* in Jewish Aramaic, in *An Aramaic Approach to the Gospels*, Third Edition (Oxford: Oxford University Press, 1967; reprint edition Peabody: Hendrickson, 1998), 329.
139. Theissen, "From the Historical Jesus to the Kerygmatic Son of God", 257, 260 (italics original).
140. The possible background to the descriptor "Son of Man", and its links to the Daniel 7:13, in Jewish Second Temple literature is a much discussed and debated topic. For an overview by a scholar who argues for the derivation of "one like a son of man" in later Jewish literature from the figure depicted in Daniel 7:13, and the linking of this figure with messianic expectations, see Benjamin E. Reynolds, *The Apocalyptic Son of Man in the Gospel of John*; WUNT 2/249 (Tübingen: Mohr Siebeck, 2008), especially chapters one and two. He extends this into an examination of New Testament literature in chapter three, and the remainder of the book deals with the Gospel of John.
141. Russell Morton, "Son of Man" in *Encyclopedia of the Historical Jesus*, edited by Craig A. Evans (New York; Abingdon, Oxon: Routledge, n.d.), 594, cites Luke 9:56 ("for the Son of Man has not come to destroy the lives of human beings but to save them") and Matthew 18:11 ("For the Son of Man came to save the lost"), both of which are not found in the best manuscripts, as evidence that not all instances of Jesus references to the Son of Man can be authentic. But even if some Son of Man sayings are to be credited to the early church (and whether one can extrapolate from these marginal instances to other cases may be debated), this would only show that the early Christians did this because they knew that the descriptor "Son of Man" had been a favoured self-reference of Jesus. That is, the balance of probability (on other evidence) tips towards most, if not all, instances in the gospels as being authentic.
142. See John P. Meier, *A Marginal Jew: Rethinking the Historical Jesus: Volume 3–Companions and Competitors* (New York: Doubleday, 2001), 131.
143. See on this, E.J. Schnabel, "Apostle" in *Dictionary of Jesus and the Gospels*, Second Edition, edited by Joel B. Green (Downers Grove/Nottingham: InterVarsity/

Inter-Varsity, 2013), 42; also Eckhard J. Schnabel, *Early Christian Mission: Volume 1, Jesus and the Twelve* (Downers Grove/Leicester: InterVarsity/Apollos, 2004), 269. Meier thinks "this solution smacks of harmonization", and offers other reasons, such as that the names of the twelve disciples were not well remembered given that they quickly lost importance as a group in the early church, or that there may have been some changes within the group over the course of Jesus's ministry (see *A Marginal Jew*, Vol. 3, 131). For lists of the twelve as found in the Synoptic Gospels and Acts, see Meier, *A Marginal Jew*, Vol. 3, 130; Schnabel, *Dictionary*, 36; *Early Christian Mission*, 263. The lists are ordered slightly differently among the gospels, and Acts.

144. In fact, two disciples, Andrew and an unnamed disciple seem to choose to follow Jesus of their own accord (John 1:35–39) and Andrew brings his brother, Simon Peter, to Jesus. Jesus appears to find Philip and asks him to follow him (John 1:43).

145. Some scholars believe that John 21 is an appendix to the Gospel added later (I do not). Here the "sons of Zebedee" (the Greek *hoi tou Zebedaiou*, "the ...of Zebedee", "the" in the plural, might be translated as "those of Zebedee"), must be assumed to be James and John.

146. Many associate "the beloved disciple" with "John the Evangelist" who is taken to be the apostle John (one of the Twelve). This may be correct: the tradition is strong. However, I prefer to think that the evangelist (viz. the Gospel's author) deliberately desired to make this disciple anonymous. You may read some of my arguments for this in my *Narrative Art and Act in the Fourth Gospel*, or, more accessibly in *Jesus: Story of God. John's Story of Jesus* (chapter two).

147. Note here the reference to Jesus choosing the Twelve (a brief acknowledgement of the Synoptic tradition?). In this exchange, however, the emphasis falls on the fact that one, Judas Iscariot, is a "devil", and will betray Jesus. Judas is named last in all the lists of the Twelve, and invariably his name is associated with a comment that he was Jesus's betrayer. I think this witnesses to the deep sense of shock the other disciples felt over his defection and betrayal.

148. I am largely drawing upon Schnabel's useful summary of the argument for this historicity of "the Twelve" in his dictionary article; see Schnabel, "Apostle", *Dictionary*, 264–65. Meier, *A Marginal Jew*, Vol. 3, 128–147, provides a much more extensive argument, drawing particularly upon the criteria of multiple attestation, and what he calls "embarrassment". Of course, one might put up counter arguments, such as the fact that "the Twelve" hardly feature as a group in the early church, and that most of the named persons in the lists hardly feature in the gospel stories, means that they never existed as a group, or that they were a literary convention (originating with Mark?), and that Judas Iscariot becomes a character who betrays Jesus as a kind of fulfilment, or "midrash" on Scripture (see e.g. Ps 41:9, cf. John 13:18). Some of Meier's arguments (and Schnabel's) might be put into reverse as it were. But the results are no more (and

in most cases less) secure than arguments for the historicity of "the Twelve" as chosen by Jesus.

149. E.P. Sanders, *The Historical Figure of Jesus* (London: Allen Lane, Penguin, 1993), 120. Schnabel, *Early Christian Mission*, 270, writes that Jesus's choice of the Twelve was a "programmatic action" (that is, one that signified the intent of his mission). He states: "[I]t designates here an action that pertains to the future and at the same time is inspired by the reality of which the symbol speaks: Jesus' calling of the twelve disciples sets in motion the expected eschatological restoration of Israel."

150. On the choosing of the twelve, see Mark 3:13–19a//Matt. 10:1–4//Luke 6:12–16 (Luke particularly notes that Jesus named the twelve "apostles"). On the sending out for mission, see Mark 6:6b–13//Matt. 9:35–10:15//Luke 9:1–6. Luke also has Jesus sending out seventy (some ancient manuscripts have "seventy-two") disciples to "every town and place where he himself intended to go" (Luke 10:1).

151. See Schnabel, "Apostle", *Dictionary*, 44.

152. Schnabel, "Apostle", *Dictionary*, 44.

153. See Birger Gerhardsson, *Memory and Manuscript: Oral Tradition and Written Transmission in Rabbinic Judaism and Early Christianity*. The Biblical Resource Series (Grand Rapids/Livonia, Mich: Eerdmans/Dove, 1998), 329–335. Gerhardsson describes the group as a *collegium*, which perhaps gives the impression of a group more organised and institutionalised than it probably was.

154. On this see Gerhardsson, *Tradition and Transmission in Early Christianity*, 40: "...the twelve and the other authoritative teachers and colleges were not traditionists only. They worked with the Word. They worked on the Scriptures, and on the Christ-tradition (which was originally oral): they gathered, formulated (narrative tradition), interpreted, adapted, developed, complemented and put together collections for various definite purposes." One need not adopt all of Gerhardsson's arguments (against which many objections have been raised), especially his contention that Jesus adopted teaching methods that were analogous to those of the (later) Rabbis. Nonetheless, Jesus was a teacher who taught in ways that were intended to be memorable, and if he was the kind of teller of parables that the Synoptic Gospels portray him as (and I believe he was) then we would be surprised if his disciples did not remember them. That goes for many of the aphorisms, riddles, and proverbial type sayings that Jesus spoke. See also Jonathan Bernier, *The Quest for the Historical Jesus After the Demise of Authenticity: Toward a Critical Realist Philosophy of History in Jesus Studies*. Library of New Testament Studies 540. (London: Bloomsbury T & T Clark, 2016), 149.

155. In theological language, "belief in Jesus as the Christ" is known as Christology and encompasses much more than simply a proclamation of Jesus as "the Messiah", and extends also to claims of Jesus's divinity, and place as the "second person" of the Trinity.

156. This Gospel also notes the selective nature of its account, see John 20:30; 21:25.
157. An impetus of early historical critical work was to get beyond the "dogmatic" intents of the early Christians.
158. Of course, a historian who is a Christian, can make that claim, but not in his capacity as a historian, but as a believer.
159. An analogy might be the description of Hitler as "evil". A historian would describe Hitler as a "tyrant", but not as "evil". However, at the popular level, and as a moral judgment, it may be an accurate representation of his personality, and the effects of his actions, to describe him as "evil".
160. Secular history aims to arrive at interpretations, or to provide a reconstruction of an event, that is potentially one that all researchers are able to accept or, at least acknowledge as valid. That is, it ought to be an "uncommitted" account. This is the impetus behind, for instance, John Meier's "unpapal conclave" (a Catholic, a Protestant, a Jew, and an agnostic) meeting to draw up a "consensus document on who Jesus of Nazareth was and what he intended in his own time and place." See John P. Meier, *A Marginal Jew: Rethinking the Historical Jesus. Volume One: The Roots of the Problem and the Person*, 1. Meier later added a Muslim to the "unpapal conclave" (see *Volume Four: Law and Love*, 12), admitting omission of a Muslim had initially been a "blind spot" (*Volume Five: Probing the Authenticity of the Parables*, fn. 10, 23–24). Of course, in truth, the "unpapal conclave" (admittedly an artificial rhetorical device, a "fantasy" wrote Meier) had one very definite "chairman", Meier himself, who had the casting vote as it were! For another, good expression of an attempt at an "uncommitted" historical account, see also E. P. Sanders, *The Historical Figure of Jesus*, Introduction.

    The question of the "objective, unbiased" nature of historiography is, of course, now regarded as a mistaken view, often dismissed as "positivistic". All historians bring their subjective judgments to the task. And there are, therefore, forms of history, such as Marxist history. But this is a large topic, and requires much more space than can be given to it here.

161. The long discourses in the John's Gospel are a special case, and are likely to be a product of later, and deep reflection by the Evangelist of aspects of Jesus's teaching, and more especially, "theological" interpretation of who Jesus is to be understood to be (which may well be a true representation of Jesus's historic significance).
162. In the light of my analysis above, I would attribute this saying to the historical Jesus, transmitted to Mark by the apostle Peter.
163. On the roots of the criteria in the work of the form critics, see Chris Keith, "The Indebtedness of the Criteria Approach to Form Criticism and Recent Attempts to Rehabilitate the Search for an Authentic Jesus", in *Jesus, Criteria, and the Demise of Authenticity*, edited by Chris Keith and Anthony Le Donne (London: T & T Clark International, 2012), 25–48. I take the word "bifurcation" from the next chapter by Jens Schröter, "The Criteria of Authenticity in

Jesus Research and Historiographical Method", 49–70. This book provides a good entrée into the issues around the criteria and the reason for their demise. Morna Hooker's *Foreword* is a particularly concise summary of the issue. See also Stanley E. Porter, *The Criteria for Authenticity in Historical-Jesus Research: Previous Discussion and New Proposals* (London: T & T Clark International, 2014), chapters one to three. This book was originally published by Sheffield Academic Press, as JSNTSup 191, in 2000.

164. Schröter, "Criteria of Authenticity", 53–54 (emphasis added). Note that Schröter uses the word "bifurcation" in respect of different scholars' approaches rather than relating to the issue of "the Jesus of history" versus "the Christ of faith" *per se*, but this issue lies behind the scholarly divide. Though I would fall into the second camp, these scholars cannot all be taken as maintaining the same thing as regards to Jesus and the kerygma. Bultmann, for instance, stated that we could know very little about the historical Jesus, but the important thing was our response to the existential call to faith and discipleship that preaching about Jesus brought.

165. See M.D. Hooker, "Christology and Methodology", *New Testament Studies* 17 (1970), 480–87 (especially on dissimilarity, 481-82); or, "On Using the Wrong Tool", *Theology* 75 (1972), 570–81 (especially 574–760); Dagmar Winter, "Saving the Quest for Authenticity from the Criterion of Dissimilarity: History and Plausibility", in *Demise*, 115–3, states that "a poor appreciation of Second Temple Judaism" is "coupled with a prejudicial anti-Judaist, if not anti-Semitic, view of Jewish religion" (124).

166. See, for his discussion of this criterion, *A Marginal Jew*, Vol. 1, 168–71.

167. See Mark 1:9–11: Mark presents a straightforward account without any apparent "embarrassment" that Jesus was baptised by John the Baptist. Matthew 3:13–17: Matthew has John object to baptising Jesus, saying that Jesus should baptise him, not vice versa. Luke 3:21–22: Luke states that John has been put in prison (v. 19), before mentioning Jesus's baptism, leaving open the question as to who baptised Jesus, and implying that it could not be John who was in prison. John's Gospel ignores, or omits, an account of Jesus's baptism altogether, and turns John the Baptist into a witness to Jesus. There is, however, a possible allusion to the Synoptic accounts in John 1:33, and see also 1:26–27. Hence reading these accounts sequentially, one gets the impression of an attempt to tone down, and avoid the implications of Mark's account.

168. Rafael Rodríguez, "The Embarrassing Truth about Jesus: The Criterion of Embarrassment and the Failure of Historical Authenticity", *Demise*, 132–51, makes a similar point about the disciples, and provides other examples of so-called "embarrassment", including the crucifixion of Jesus which Paul describes as "a stumbling block to Jews and foolishness to Greeks" (1 Cor. 1:23) but which the early Christians make central to their proclamation of the Christ.

169. The phrase "of course", is, of course (!), this translation's rendering of the Greek, which more literally may be translated: "for John had not yet been thrown into prison" (cf. RSV).
170. On difficulties, or problems, with the criteria of multiple attestation, and coherence, as items in the suite of tools as traditionally used among scholars, see the contributions by Anthony Le Donne and Mark Goodacre in *Jesus, Criteria, and the Demise of Authenticity*.
171. Gerd Theissen and Dagmar Winter, *The Quest for the Plausible Jesus: The Question of Criteria*. Translated by M. Eugene Boring (Louisville: Westminster John Knox, 2002), 209. The first aspect, placing Jesus plausibly within his Jewish context, they call "contextual plausibility", see especially pp. 179–88, and pp. 206–07 (for a useful summary). The second aspect they refer to as "plausibility of historical effects", see pp. 173–79, also 207–09.
172. Theissen and Winter, *Quest*, 172.
173. At the outset of their discussion on the criterion of historical plausibility, they point out that the application of the criterion of dissimilarity by scholars of the "New Quest" applied the criterion "only weakly with regard to Christianity, since there was a conscious effort to develop a continuity between the historical Jesus and earliest Christianity" (172). The converse happened with regards to Judaism, as Jesus was seen to be set apart from Judaism. Over against these tendencies, Theissen and Winter place Jesus more firmly within his Jewish context, but distance Jesus from the early Christians, or rather the history (or development) of the traditions about Jesus tended to carry the tradition about Jesus "further and further from Jesus" (174). Their arguments are subtle and at times a little difficult to follow, and in places seem contradictory. They provide a summary of their argument on pp. 210–212, in which they lay out the overall characteristics of the criterion of historical plausibility. Here the "bottom line", if you will, is that the reconstruction that emerges must provide a comprehensive picture of the historical Jesus, which seems to suggest that a general, broad brush picture is better than a detailed one. They include here this sentence (italicized in the original): *"What we know of Jesus as a whole must allow him to be recognized within his contemporary Jewish context and must be compatible with the Christian (canonical and non-canonical) history of his effects"* (212). One has to understand, however, that the Christian "history of his effects" that the historical Jesus must be compatible with, are those that survive a paring away of Christian theological tendencies and interpretations of Jesus.
174. N.T. Wright, *Jesus and the Victory of God;* Volume Two of Christian Origins and the Question of God series (London: SPCK, 1996), 132.
175. Porter, *Criteria for Authenticity*, Part Two.
176. Of course, the analogy falls down in that an archaeologist can recover actual physical artefacts, whereas the historian can only reconstruct a conjectural historical figure.

177. See the collection of essays in Alan Kirk and Tom Thatcher, eds. *Memory, Tradition, and Text: Uses of the Past in Early Christianity,* Semeia Studies 52 (Altanta: Society of Biblical Literature, 2005). On the "presentist" mode, see Barry Schwartz's essay (on p. 44). As examples of the creation of memories out of Scripture, or typological functions, see in particular the essays by Arthur J. Dewey and Antionette Clark Wire. Interestingly, and in connection with the argument I am making in this manifesto, Barry Schwartz, in a second concluding contribution critiquing some omissions in the essays, writes this: "That two of these essays deal with the crucifixion, but none with the resurrection, is a major shortcoming, for the conviction that God raised Jesus is the foundation of belief in Jesus' divinity and messianic mission. A second shortcoming stems from the authors' conveying such a strong sense of Christianity's inevitability. Resurrection preserved belief in Jesus' claim to be the world's Messiah, but none of our authors attempt to explain why so precarious a claim could have spread as rapidly and deeply as it did." (258) While he may overstate what Jesus's claim might have been, I find it intriguing that a sociologist picks up on a fundamental point that so many biblical scholars miss.
178. See e.g. Georgia Masters Keightley's contribution in Kirk and Thatcher, *Memory,* 129–150. A scholar who examines the operations of memory, and places more faith in the "collective memory' found in the gospels as containing reasonably true memories of the life and teaching of the historical Jesus is Robert K. McIver, *Memory, Jesus, and the Synoptic Gospels.* Resources for Biblical Study 59 (Atlanta: Society of Biblical Literature, 2011).
179. For Dunn's argument, see *Jesus Remembered,* Chapter Eight. *Haflat Samar* is a term for the gatherings in Middle Eastern villages where peasant men gather at night to pass on stories and poems as a way of preserving the traditions of their community.
180. Dunn, *Jesus Remembered,* 223. Dunn provides a number of examples where it is evident the same story is being told. The pericopes analysed synoptically show quite a variation in the wording, although some parts are word for word: these are usually a "punchline" saying or important element in the story, though some are incidental words and phrases, or demanded by the nature of the content. His argument is that as the traditions were passed on orally, each retelling was a new performance (rather than arising from literary redaction). This makes sense, although it is not necessarily a clear case that the variations arise from oral retelling and are not due to the evangelist's literary shaping in light of thematic and theological interests. For Dunn's argument, see *Jesus Remembered,* Chapter Eight.
181. Dunn places more emphasis upon "oral tradition" than I do in this work. For his emphasis on the place of memory and "community tradition" (by which he means the oral tradition as much as the tradition as written in the Synoptic gospels), see *Jesus Remembered,* 329, 335.

182. Morna D. Hooker, "Forward: Forty Years On", *Demise*, xv.
183. Theissen and Winter, *Quest*, 227.
184. Theissen himself seems to walk this back when later providing a "philosophical" reason for the hypothetical character of our knowledge. He writes, "Everything is hypothetical, penultimate, and in need of improvement. And precisely for this reason we can come to terms with the hypothetical character of our knowledge *and our faith.*" (259, emphasis added).
185. Scot McKnight, "Why the Authentic Jesus is of No Use for the Church", *Demise*, 173–185, makes similar points. He also claims that *"Historical Jesus study is a kind of theology because every reconstruction of Jesus in theological."*(175, emphasis original). He states that "The remembered Jesus…is the church's Jesus" (184). Much that he writes bears pondering, but if the implication is that, the "remembered Jesus" as "the church's Jesus", need not also stand alongside the other Jesuses as a "plausible" Jesus, or that we should not attempt to make a case for the historical Jesus of the gospels to stand alongside other reconstructions as a plausible alternative, I would demur.

BIBLIOGRAPHY

Allison, Dale C. *Resurrecting Jesus: The Earliest Christian Tradition and Its Interpreters*. New York/London: T & T Clark International, 2005.

Bauckham, Richard. *Jesus and the Eyewitnesses: The Gospels as Eyewitness Testimony*. Grand Rapids: Eerdmans, 2006.

Bernier, Jonathan. *Rethinking the Dates of the New Testament: The Evidence of Early Composition*. Grand Rapids: Baker Academic, 2022.

Bernier, Jonathan. *The Quest for the Historical Jesus After the Demise of Authenticity: Toward a Critical Realist Philosophy of History in Jesus Studies*. LNTS 540. London: Bloomsbury, 2016.

Bird, Michael F., Craig A. Evans, Simon J. Gathercole, Charles E. Hill, Chris Tilling. *How God Became Jesus: The Real Origins of Belief in Jesus' Divine Nature–A Response to Bart Ehrman*. Grand Rapids: Zondervan, 2014.

Black, Matthew. *An Aramaic Approach to the Gospels and Acts*. Third Edition, with an Introduction by Craig A. Evans and an Appendix by Geza Vermes. 1967. Repr. Peabody, MA: Hendrickson, 1998.

Bock, Darrell L. and Robert L. Webb, eds. *Key Events in the Life of the Historical Jesus: A Collaborative Exploration of Context and Coherence*. Grand Rapids: Eerdmans, 2010.

Bockmuehl, Markus, ed. *The Cambridge Companion to Jesus*. Cambridge: Cambridge University Press, 2001.

Bockmuehl, Markus, "Resurrection". Pages 102–118 in *Cambridge Companion to Jesus*. Edited by Markus Bockmuehl. Cambridge: Cambridge University Press, 2001.

Bond, Helen K. *The Historical Jesus: A Guide for the Perplexed*. London/New York: T & T Clark International, 2012.

Borg, Marcus J. *Jesus, A New Vision: Spirit, Culture and the Life of Discipleship*. London: SPCK, 1993.

Borg, Marcus J. *Meeting Jesus Again for the First Time: The Historical Jesus & the Heart of Contemporary Faith*. New York: HarperCollins, 1995.

Bultmann, Rudolf. *The History of the Synoptic Tradition*. Revised Edition. Translated by John Marsh. Oxford: Basil Blackwell, 1963. Repr. Peabody, MA: Hendrickson, n.d.

Bultmann, Rudolf. *Theology of the New Testament.* Volume One. Translated by Kendrick Grobel. New York: Charles Scribner's Sons, 1951.

Carr, E.H. *What is History?* Harmondsworth, Middx: Penguin Books, 1964 (originally published by Macmillan, 1961).

Chilton, Bruce. "(The) Son of (the) Man, and Jesus." Pages 259–287 in *Authenticating the Words of Jesus.* Edited by Bruce Chilton and Craig. A. Evans. Leiden: Brill, 2002.

Collingwood, R.G. *The Idea of History.* Revised Edition, with Lectures 1926–1928. Edited with an Introduction by Jan Van Der Dussen. Oxford: Oxford University Press, 1994.

Collins, Adela Yarbro. "Son of Man." Pages 341–348 in *The New Interpreter's Dictionary of the Bible S-Z.* Volume Five. Edited by Katharine Doob Sakenfeld, et. al. Nashville: Abingdon, 2009.

Collins, Adela Yarbro. *Mark: A Commentary.* Hermeneia. Minneapolis: Fortress, 2007.

Crossan, John Dominic. *The Historical Jesus: The Life of a Mediterranean Jewish Peasant.* New York: HarperCollins, 1991.

Dahl, N.A. "Kerygma and History." Pages 131–144 in *In Search of The Historical Jesus.* Edited by Harvey K McArthur. London: SPCK, 1970.

Dodd, C.H. *The Parables of the Kingdom.* Fount Paperbacks. Glasgow: Collins, 1978.

Dunn, James D. G. *A New Perspective on Jesus: What the Quest for the Historical Jesus Missed.* Grand Rapids: Baker Academic, 2005.

Dunn, James D. G. *Did the First Christians Worship Jesus? The New Testament Evidence.* London: SPCK; Louisville: Westminster John Knox, 2010.

Dunn, James D. G. *Jesus Remembered.* Vol. 1 of *Christianity in the Making.* Grand Rapids: Eerdmans, 2003.

Dunn, James D. G. *The Oral Gospel Tradition.* Grand Rapids: Eerdmans, 2013.

Ehrman, Bart D. *How Jesus Became God: The Exaltation of a Jewish Preacher from Galilee.* New York: HarperCollins, 2014.

Elton, G.R. *The Practice of History.* The Fontana Library. London & Glasgow: Collins, 1969 (first published Sydney University Press, 1967).

Endsjo, Dag Oistein. *Greek Resurrection Beliefs and the Success of Christianity.* New York: Palgrave MacMillan, 2009.

Eusebius, *The Ecclesiastical History.* Volume One. With an English Translation by Kirsopp Lake. LCL Cambridge, MA: Harvard University Press; London: William Heinemann, 1926.

Fosdick, Harry Emerson. *The Man from Nazareth.* London: SCM, 1950.

Gallie, W.B. *Philosophy and the Historical Understanding.* Second Edition. New York: Schocken Books, 1968.

Gerhardsson, Birger. *Memory & Manuscript: Oral Tradition and Written Transmission in Rabbinic Judaism and Early Christianity* with *Tradition and Transmission in Early Christianity*. The Biblical Resource Series. Grand Rapids: Eerdmans; Livonia, MI: Dove Booksellers, 1998.

Gnilka, Joachim. *Jesus of Nazareth: Message and History*. Translated by Siegfried S. Schatzmann. Peabody, MA: Hendrickson, 1997.

Guelich, Robert A. *Mark 1–8:26*. Word Biblical Commentary 34A. Nashville: Thomas Nelson, 1989.

Hays, Richard B. *First Corinthians*. Interpretation. Louisville: John Knox, 1997.

Hengel, Martin. *The Four Gospels and the One Gospel of Jesus Christ: An Investigation of the Collection and Origin of the Canonical Gospels*. Translated by John Bowden. London: SCM, 2000.

Hooker, M. D. "Christology and Methodology." *New Testament Studies* 17 (1970): 480–87.

Hooker, M.D. "On Using the Wrong Tool." *Theology* 75 (1972): 570–81.

Hoskyns, Edwyn and Noel Davey. *The Riddle of the New Testament*. London: Faber and Faber, 1958.

Hurtado, Larry W. *At the Origins of Christian Worship: The Context and Character of Earliest Christian Devotion*. Grand Rapids: Eerdmans, 1999.

Hurtado, Larry W. *How on Earth Did Jesus Become a God? Historical Questions about Earliest Devotion to Jesus*. Grand Rapids: Eerdmans, 2005.

Hurtado, Larry W. *Lord Jesus Christ: Devotion to Jesus in Earliest Christianity*. Grand Rapids: Eerdmans, 2003.

Hurtado, Larry W. *One God, One Lord: Early Christian Devotion and Ancient Jewish Monotheism*. Philadelphia, 1988.

Keith, Chris and Anthony Le Donne, *Jesus, Criteria and the Demise of Authenticity*. London: T & T Clark, 2012.

Kinman, Brent. "Jesus' Royal Entry into Jerusalem." Pages 383–427 in *Key Events in the Life of the Historical Jesus*. Edited by Darrell L. Bock and Robert L. Webb. Grand Rapids: Eerdmans, 2010.

Köstenberger, Andreas J. "John". Pages 415–512 in *Commentary on the New Testament Use of the Old Testament*. Edited by G.K. Beale and D.A. Carson. Grand Rapids: Baker Academic; Nottingham: Apollos/Inter-Varsity Press, 2007.

Lindars, Barnabas. "Son of Man." Pages 639–642 in *A Dictionary of Biblical Interpretation*. Edited by R.J. Coggins and J.L. Houlden. London: SCM; Philadelphia, PA: Trinity Press International, 1990.

Lord, Albert B. *The Singer of Tales*. Harvard Studies in Comparative Literature. Cambridge, MA: Harvard University Press, 1960.

Meier, John P. *A Marginal Jew: Rethinking the Historical Jesus. Volume One: The Roots of the Problem and the Person*. The Anchor Bible Reference Library. New York: Doubleday, 1991.

Meier, John P. *A Marginal Jew: Rethinking the Historical Jesus. Volume Two: Mentor, Message, and Miracles*. The Anchor Bible Reference Library. New York: Doubleday, 1994.

Meier, John P. *A Marginal Jew: Rethinking the Historical Jesus. Volume Three: Companions and Competitors.* The Anchor Bible Reference Library. New York: Doubleday, 2001.

Meier, John P. *A Marginal Jew: Rethinking the Historical Jesus. Volume Five: Probing the Authenticity of the Parables.* The Anchor Yale Bible Reference Library. New Haven: Yale University Press, 2016.

Osborne, Grant R. "Jesus' Empty Tomb and His Appearance in Jerusalem." Pages 775–823 in *Key Events in the Life of the Historical Jesus.* Edited by Darrell L. Bock and Robert L. Webb. Grand Rapids: Eerdmans, 2010.

Perrin, N. "Last Supper." Pages 492–501 in *Dictionary of Jesus and the Gospels.* Second Edition. Edited by Joel B. Green, Jeannine K. Brown and Nicholas Perrin. Downers Grove, IL: InterVarsity Press; Nottingham: Inter-Varsity Press, 2013.

Porter, Stanley E. *The Criteria for Authenticity in Historical-Jesus Research: Previous Discussion and New Proposals.* London: T & T Clark International, 2004.

Pratt, Mary Louise. *Toward a Speech Act Theory of Literary Discourse.* Bloomington. IL: Indiana University Press, 1977.

Rae, Murray A. *History and Hermeneutics.* London: T & T Clark, 2005.

Robinson, John A. T. *Redating the New Testament.* London: SCM, 1976.

Sampley, J. Paul. "The First Letter to the Corinthians." Pages 773–1003 in *The New Interpreter's Bible.* Volume X. Edited by Leander E. Keck, et. al. Nashville: Abingdon, 2002.

Sanders, E.P. *Jesus and Judaism.* London: SCM, 1985.

Sanders, E.P. *The Historical Figure of Jesus.* Harmondsworth, Middx: Penguin, 1993.

Schnabel, E. J. "Apostle." Pages 34–45 in *Dictionary of Jesus and the Gospels.* Edited by Joel B. Green, Jeannine K. Brown and Nicholas Perrin. Downers Grove, IL: InterVarsity Press; Nottingham: Inter-Varsity Press, 2013.

Schnabel, Eckhard J. *Early Christian Mission. Volume One: Jesus and the Twelve.* Downers Grove, IL: InterVarsity; Leicester: Apollos/Inter-Varsity, 2004.

Schweitzer, Albert. *The Quest of the Historical Jesus.* Translated by W. Montgomery, J. R. Coates, Susan Cupitt, and John Bowden. First Complete Edition edited by John Bowden. Minneapolis: Fortress, 2001.

Talbert, Charles H., ed. *Reimarus: Fragments.* Translated by Ralph S. Fraser. Lives of Jesus Series. London: SCM, 1971.

The Apostolic Fathers: Greek Texts and English Translations. Third Edition. Edited and Translated by Michael W. Holmes. Grand Rapids: Baker Academic, 2007.

The Five Gospels: The Search for the Authentic Words of Jesus. New Translation and Commentary by Robert W. Funk, Roy W. Hoover and the Jesus Seminar. New York: Macmillan/Polebridge, 1993.

The Kalevala: An Epic Poem after Oral Tradition by Elias Lönnrot. Translated from the Finnish with an Introduction and Notes by Keith Bosley. The World's Classics. Oxford: Oxford University Press, 1989.

The New Complete Works of Josephus. Translated by William Whiston. Revised and Expanded Edition. Grand Rapids: Kregel, 1999.

The New Interpreter's Study Bible: New Revised Standard Version with the Apocrypha. Edited by Walter J. Harrelson (Gen. Ed.), Donald Senior, Abraham Smith, Phyllis Trible, James C. VanderKam. Nashville: Abingdon, 2003.

Theissen, Gerd. "From the Historical Jesus to the Kerygmatic Son of God: How Role Analysis Contributes to the Understanding of New Testament Christology." Pages 235–260 in *Jesus Research: New Methodologies and Perceptions. The Second Princeton-Prague Symposium on Jesus Research, Princeton 2007*. Princeton-Prague Symposia Series on the Historical Jesus. Edited by James H. Charlesworth with Brian Rhea. Grand Rapids: Eerdmans, 2014.

Theissen, Gerd and Annette Merz. *The Historical Jesus: A Comprehensive Guide*. Translated by John Bowden. Minneapolis: Fortress, 1998.

Theissen, Gerd and Dagmar Winter. *The Quest for the Plausible Jesus: The Question of Criteria*. Translated by M. Eugene Boring. Louisville: Westminster John Knox, 2002.

Tovey, Derek. *Jesus, Story of God: John's Story of Jesus*. Hindmarsh, SA: ATF Press, 2007.

Tovey, Derek. *Narrative Art and Act in the Fourth Gospel*. JSNTSup 151. Sheffield: Sheffield Academic, 1997.

Tovey, Derek. *Read Mark and Learn: Following Mark's Jesus*. Eugene, OR: Wipf & Stock, 2014.

Vermes, Geza. *Jesus the Jew: A Historian's Reading of the Gospels*. London: Collins, 1973.

Vermes, Geza. *Jesus in His Jewish Context*. London: SCM, 2003.

Wright N.T. *Jesus and the Victory of God*. Vol. 2 of *Christian Origins and the Question of God*. London: SPCK, 1996.

Wright. N.T. *The Resurrection of the Son of God*. Vol. 3 of *Christian Origins and the Question of God*. Minneapolis: Fortress, 2003.

Now retired, Derek Tovey taught New Testament at The College of St. John the Evangelist (Auckland, New Zealand) for twenty-one years, and as an honorary lecturer at the University of Auckland, first within the Auckland Consortium for Theological Education, and then in the School of Theology. He had previously completed a doctoral degree at Durham University, UK, in 1994, entitled *Narrative Art and Act in the Fourth Gospel*. This was subsequently published in 1997, by Sheffield Academic Press (JSNTSup 151). He is the author of two other books, and a number of book chapters and journal articles.

www.ingramcontent.com/pod-product-compliance
Lightning Source LLC
Chambersburg PA
CBHW051450290426
44109CB00016B/1690